GRAMMAR WORKBOOK

EXERCISES in ENGLISH

LEVEL F

LOYOLAPRESS.

CHICAGO

Consultants
Therese Elizabeth Bauer
Martina Anne Erdlen
Anita Patrick Gallagher
Patricia Healey
Irene Kervick
Susan Platt

Linguistics Advisor
Timothy G. Collins
National-Louis University

Series Design: Loyola Press
Interior Art:
Jim Mitchell: 2, 19, 21, 42, 63, 87, 104, 109, 126.
Greg Phillips: 12, 51, 78, 80, 136.
All interior illustrations not listed above are by Mona Mark/Represented by Anita Grien.

ISBN-10: 0-8294-2338-9; ISBN-13: 978-0-8294-2338-9

Exercises in English® is a registered trademark of Loyola Press.

Manufactured in the United States of America.

06 07 08 09 10 11 12 VonH 10 9 8 7 6 5 4 3 2 1

Table of Contents

Name _____

1. Singular Nouns and Plural Nouns

A noun is a name word. A **singular noun** names one person, place, or thing. A **plural noun** names more than one person, place, or thing. Add *-s* to form the plurals of most nouns. Add *-es* to form the plurals of most nouns ending in *s, x, z, ch,* or *sh.* Some plural nouns are not formed by adding *-s* or *-es.* Check a dictionary if you are not sure of a plural form.

SINGULAR	PLURAL	SINGULAR	PLURAL
boat	**boats**	**fox**	**foxes**
man	**men**	**fish**	**fish**

A. Write the plural form of each word.

1. batch _batchs_
2. cow _cows_
3. moose _moose_
4. bush _____
5. tooth _____
6. princess _____
7. foot _____
8. ditch _____
9. woman _____
10. mile _____

11. computer _____
12. compass _____
13. house _____
14. trout _____
15. series _____
16. ox _____
17. rabbit _____
18. mouse _____
19. book _____
20. tax _____

B. Complete each sentence with the plural form of the noun.

piece   1. Pack both _____ of watermelon into the cooler.

child   2. Many _____ begin their education in preschool.

box   3. How many moving _____ did your family buy?

sheep   4. We saw six _____ at the fair.

refugee   5. The _____ fled to a neighboring country.

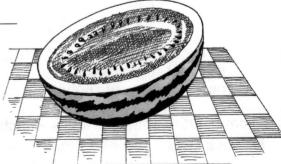

2. More Singular Nouns and Plural Nouns

If a noun ends in *y* preceded by a vowel, form the plural by adding *-s*. If a noun ends in *y* preceded by a consonant, change the *y* to *i* and add *-es*.

SINGULAR	PLURAL	SINGULAR	PLURAL
valley	valleys	colony	colonies

If a noun ends in *o* preceded by a vowel, form the plural by adding *-s*. If a noun ends in *o* preceded by a consonant, form the plural by adding *-es*. There are exceptions to this rule, so consult a dictionary to be sure.

SINGULAR	PLURAL	SINGULAR	PLURAL
radio	radios	tomato	tomatoes
video	videos	taco	tacos

For most nouns ending in *f* or *fe,* form the plurals by adding *-s*. For some nouns ending in *f* or *fe,* change the *f* or *fe* to *ves*. Check a dictionary if necessary.

SINGULAR	PLURAL	SINGULAR	PLURAL
roof	roofs	leaf	leaves

Complete each sentence with the plural form of the noun.

inventor 1. Thomas Edison is one of America's most important ___inventors___.

life 2. His inventions changed people's ___lifes___.

assistant 3. Edison had a team of ___assistants___.

supply 4. He provided the _____ they needed to work.

movie 5. Edison invented the cameras, film, and projectors that made _____ possible.

battery 6. He also developed a better way to make _____.

factory 7. Edison designed and built many kinds of _____.

torpedo 8. During World War I, he helped the U.S. military forces build _____.

key 9. One of the _____ to Edison's success was reading. Before he began a project, he read a lot about the subject.

day 10. Three _____ after Edison died, much of America dimmed its lights for one minute in his honor.

Thomas Edison always read as much as he could before he started a new project. Give an example of a way you can use reading to help yourself.

3. Count Nouns and Noncount Nouns

Count nouns name things that can be counted. Count nouns have singular and plural forms. **Noncount nouns** name things that cannot be counted. Noncount nouns do not have plural forms.

COUNT	NONCOUNT		COUNT	NONCOUNT
suitcases	luggage		chairs	furniture
lemons	lemonade		emotions	anger

Some nouns can be count or noncount.
He baked two <u>pies</u>. (count)   **He had <u>pie</u> for dessert.** (noncount)

A. Circle each count noun. Underline each noncount noun.

1. The ancient Aztecs inhabited what is now Mexico.

2. Farmers in the highlands grew corn.

3. They traded their grain for things from the lowlands.

4. Artisans made jewelry out of gold and silver.

5. Potters made beautiful jars out of clay.

6. The Aztecs did not have an alphabet.

7. They used pictographs to write stories.

8. The Aztecs studied the sun, the moon, and the stars.

9. They developed a calendar based on these bodies.

10. Their calendar had 365 days in a year.

11. The people planted gardens on islands made of mud.

12. Trees were planted to hold the soil together.

13. The Aztecs built magnificent temples in honor of their gods.

14. The temples were in the shape of pyramids.

15. People today show admiration for these accomplishments.

B. Complete each sentence with a noun. Write **C** if it is a count noun or **N** if it is a noncount noun.

_____ 1. Farmers in my state raise _____.

_____ 2. A factory near here manufactures _____.

_____ 3. I often buy _____ at the supermarket.

_____ 4. I can make _____ if I want to.

_____ 5. I like to eat _____.

4. Concrete Nouns and Abstract Nouns

A **concrete noun** names a thing that can be seen or touched.

The Greek temple is at the top of a mountain.

An **abstract noun** expresses a quality or a condition. It names something that cannot be seen or touched. Abstract nouns can be formed from other words by adding suffixes such as -*dom*, -*hood*, -*ion*, -*tion*, -*ity*, -*ment*, -*ness*, -*ry*, -*ship*, -*th*, and -*ty*.

Democracy had its origin in ancient Greece.

A. Underline the concrete nouns in each sentence. Circle the abstract nouns.

1. People in ancient times had differing values and beliefs.

2. Some Greek kingdoms valued toughness and discipline.

3. All authority in these governments was held by the king.

4. The army was extremely important in keeping order.

5. Slaves and peasants farmed the land and had few rights.

6. Other Greek societies believed in freedom and democracy.

7. They valued truth, beauty, and order.

8. Their citizens erected beautiful buildings and statues.

9. Plato, a Greek philosopher, wrote about democratic principles.

10. His most famous book is *The Republic*.

B. Write an abstract noun for each word by adding a suffix.

1. good _____   6. leader _____

2. brave _____   7. entertain _____

3. friend _____   8. appreciate _____

4. king _____   9. accomplish _____

5. grow _____   10. honest _____

5. Nouns Used as Subjects

A noun can be the subject of a verb. The **subject** tells what the sentence is about.

The Trojan War, fought by two ancient city-states, is the subject of a famous legend.

During the war Greek soldiers from Sparta attacked Troy.

A. Underline the subject in each sentence.

1. Menelaus was the king of Sparta.

2. His wife's name was Helen.

3. His wife fell in love with a prince from Troy and followed him there.

4. According to legend, the Greeks started a war against Troy.

5. The war lasted more than 11 years.

6. Finally, a Greek soldier suggested a tactic.

7. His plan was to build a large wooden statue of a horse.

8. Greek soldiers hid inside the horse.

9. The Greek army left the horse near the gates of Troy and sailed away.

10. The people found the statue and took it into the city.

11. A woman of Troy tried to warn the people about the statue.

12. Cassandra's warnings were ignored.

13. The ships carrying the Greeks returned that night.

14. The troops inside the horse emerged and opened the city gates.

15. Troy lost the war because of this surprise attack by the Greeks.

B. Use each noun as the subject of a sentence.

1. Greece _____

2. Troy _____

3. legend _____

4. Cassandra _____

5. the Trojan horse _____

6. Nouns Used as Subject Complements

> A noun can be used as a subject complement. A **subject complement** is a noun that completes the meaning of a linking verb in a sentence. It renames or describes the subject. The most common linking verbs are forms of the verb *be* (*is, am, are, was, were,* and so on).
>
> **Japan is a country in Asia.** (country = Japan)

A. Underline each subject complement.

1. Japan is a country of islands.

2. Korea, China, and Russia are the nearest neighbors of Japan.

3. The capital of Japan is Tokyo.

4. Tokyo is a large, densely populated city.

5. The official language of the country is Japanese.

6. In the Japanese language the name of the country is not Japan.

7. The name in Japanese is Nippon.

8. Of Japan's four major islands, the biggest is Honshu.

9. Many of the Japanese people are farmers and fishers.

10. Rice is an important crop in Japan.

11. Fish, both fresh and canned, is an important product.

12. Japan, however, is not primarily an agricultural country.

13. Japan is a major industrial country.

14. It is a notable producer of cars, electronics, and machines.

15. In fact, Japan is a major economic power.

B. Circle the subject in each sentence. Underline the subject complement.

1. Japan is a mountainous country.

2. Some of its mountains are volcanoes.

3. The most famous volcano in Japan is Mount Fuji.

4. This mountain is the subject of many works of art.

5. A climb to the top of Mount Fuji is an important goal of many Japanese.

Name _____

7. Nouns Used as Direct Objects

A noun can be used as the direct object of a verb. A **direct object** answers the question *whom* or *what* after the verb.

| VERB | DIRECT OBJECT | | VERB | DIRECT OBJECT |

Britain acquired Hong Kong in the 1800s. It ruled the colony until 1997.

A. Circle the direct object(s) in each sentence. The verbs are *italicized*.

1. Hong Kong *includes* some 200 islands off the south coast of China.

2. Britain *leased* this territory from China in 1898.

3. Hong Kong *reclaimed* land from the sea to gain more space.

4. Hong Kong *traded* goods with the rest of China until 1949.

5. At that time Britain *forbade* trade with Communist China.

6. Since the 1960s Hong Kong *has manufactured* many goods for trade.

7. For more than 30 years China *requested* the return of Hong Kong.

8. Britain officially *returned* the land to China on July 1, 1997.

9. Now the People's Republic of China *governs* Hong Kong.

10. By Chinese law Hong Kong *will have* a capitalist economy for several decades.

B. Underline the verb in each sentence. Circle each direct object.

1. An emperor of China, Qin Shi Huang, began the Great Wall in 221 BC.

2. The builders used brick, stone, and soil for the wall.

3. The wall protected the country's border.

4. It kept enemies out of China.

5. Guards on the wall built fires.

6. Smoke from a fire warned people about enemies in the area.

7. Through the use of satellites, scientists studied the wall.

8. With the satellite data they discovered more sections below ground.

9. The Chinese government has plans for wall repairs as necessary.

10. Today the wall amazes tourists from all over the world.

7

8. Nouns Used as Indirect Objects

> A noun can be used as the indirect object of a verb. An **indirect object** tells *to whom, for whom, to what,* or *for what* the action was done.
>
> | VERB | INDIRECT OBJECT | DIRECT OBJECT |
> |------|-----------------|---------------|
> | Iris taught | the old dog | new tricks. |

A. Underline the verb in each sentence. Circle the indirect object. The direct object is *italicized*.

1. The hospital volunteer read the patient a *story*.
2. The school committee awarded Marjorie a *prize* for her essay.
3. Mrs. Jones bought her son a new *bicycle*.
4. I sent the editor a *letter* about a new park for our neighborhood.
5. The museum offered the owner a million *dollars* for the painting.
6. The soloist sang the audience a beautiful *ballad*.
7. Mrs. Williamson told the children a *story* about visiting the Kremlin.
8. The music teacher taught the class a patriotic *song*.
9. George Washington told people the *truth*.
10. Tyrone gave his mother some *roses* on Mother's Day.

B. Complete each sentence with a noun used as an indirect object. Underline the direct object.

1. The teacher gave _____ their homework assignment.
2. The U.S. Constitution guarantees _____ the right to vote.
3. The movie star sent _____ an autographed picture.
4. Their father promised _____ pizza for dinner.
5. Ms. Gibbs was pleased with the service at the hotel, so she wrote _____ a complimentary letter.
6. The press secretary handed _____ a copy of the president's speech.
7. Mr. Glass sent _____ an order for 10 books.
8. The instructor taught _____ the rules of the road.
9. The guide showed _____ the desk where the president worked.
10. The usher offered _____ a program with information about the play.

9. Nouns Used as Objects of Prepositions

> A noun can be used as the object of a preposition. Prepositions show time, direction, place, and relationship. Some common prepositions are *in, into, on, to, by, for, from, at, with,* and *without.* The noun that follows a preposition in a prepositional phrase is called the **object of the preposition;** it answers *whom* or *what* after the preposition.
>
> | PREPOSITION | OBJECT | PREPOSITION | OBJECT |
> |---|---|---|---|
> | **Venice is located on** | **islands** | **that are in the** | **Adriatic Sea.** |

A. Circle each object of a preposition. The prepositions are *italicized.*

1. Venice is a city *in* Italy, a country *of* southern Europe.
2. Venice was an important port *during* the Middle Ages.
3. Venetian merchants traded *with* many different countries.
4. Venetian ships traveled *between* Italy and the Middle East.
5. Marco Polo, the famous explorer *of* China, was *from* Venice.
6. Today Venice is famous *for* beautiful buildings.
7. The Rialto Bridge passes *over* the Grand Canal *in* the center *of* the city.
8. Cars cannot be driven *into* Venice, so *outside* the city are parking lots.
9. People travel *through* the city *on* vaporettos, which are water buses.
10. Tourists ride *in* gondolas, small boats paddled *by* large oars.

B. Complete each sentence with prepositions.

1. _____ 1271 Marco Polo traveled _____ China.
2. _____ the trip he passed _____ Turkey, Iran, and Afghanistan.
3. His party traveled _____ boat, _____ foot, and _____ camels.
4. Marco Polo stayed _____ China _____ 17 years.
5. He met people _____ China, India, Mongolia, and other countries.
6. He worked _____ the emperor _____ China, Kublai Khan.
7. After returning _____ Italy, he wrote a book _____ the trip.
8. Many people _____ Italy didn't believe his amazing stories _____ China.
9. Marco Polo's book has been translated _____ many languages.
10. He may be the most famous traveler _____ the history _____ the world!

10. Possessive Nouns

A **possessive noun** expresses possession or ownership. The singular possessive is formed by adding -'s after the singular noun. The plural possessive is formed by adding an apostrophe after the final s of a regular plural noun or by adding -'s after an irregular plural noun.

A. For each noun write these forms: singular possessive, plural, and plural possessive. Use a dictionary if necessary.

	SINGULAR POSSESSIVE	PLURAL	PLURAL POSSESSIVE
1. turkey	turkey's	turkeys	turkeys'
2. neighbor	neighbor's	neighbors	neighbors'
3. driver	driver's	drivers	drivers'
4. sheep			
5. child			
6. fox			
7. teacher			
8. woman			
9. man			
10. sister-in-law			

B. Rewrite each phrase, using a possessive noun.

1. the orders of the coach _____

2. a delay of an hour _____

3. the home of my parents _____

4. the books of the teacher _____

5. the toys of the children _____

11. More Possessive Nouns

Notice how the singular and plural possessives are formed.

	SINGULAR	PLURAL
REGULAR	student's desk	students' desks
IRREGULAR	man's car	men's cars

A. Complete each sentence with the possessive form of the noun.

pilot   1. A ____pilot's____ training requires long hours of hard study.

Sally   2. ____Sally's____ running shoes are in the upstairs closet.

soldiers   3. We listened to the rhythmic sound of the ____soldiers'____ feet as the group marched.

Mrs. Riddle   4. Tina and Sue washed _____ car.

boys   5. The _____ books are in their backpacks.

women   6. _____ coats are on sale this week.

Thomas   7. Did you find _____ in-line skates?

brother-in-law   8. On Thanksgiving Day we tasted my _____ special sweet potatoes.

deer   9. The _____ large antlers show that it is quite old.

guards   10. The security _____ office is near the exit.

B. Rewrite each phrase, using a possessive noun.

1. the request of the librarian   _____

2. the work of three scientists   _____

3. the diagnosis of the doctor   _____

4. the bicycles of the girls   _____

5. the cell phones of the workers   _____

6. the shouts of our children   _____

7. a pen of Mr. James   _____

8. the red feathers of the cardinals   _____

9. the statements of some witnesses   _____

10. the suitcases of my guests   _____

Nouns

12. Nouns Showing Separate and Joint Possession

Separate possession occurs when two or more people own things independently. **Joint possession** occurs when two or more people own something together. To show separate possession, use -'s after each noun. To show joint possession, use -'s after the last noun only.

> Carl and Peter each did a project. <u>Carl's</u> and <u>Peter's</u> projects are completed.
>
> Mary and Lisa did a project together. Mary and <u>Lisa's</u> project is completed.

A. Read each sentence. On the line write **S** if separate possession is shown or **J** if joint possession is shown.

____J____ 1. Jim and Karen's project was a model of an Aztec pyramid.

____S____ 2. Laura's and Tom's projects are on the table in the hall.

____J____ 3. Ken and Susan's report is on Benjamin Franklin.

_____ 4. Leo and Pablo's assignment was a map of the Oregon Trail.

_____ 5. Lou's and Marta's presentations were excellent.

B. Read each pair of sentences. Combine each pair into a single sentence that shows separate or joint possession.

1. Ron and Ella have a poodle. It won the dog show.

_____

2. Misha and Harriet each have a dachshund. They were the friendliest dogs in the show.

_____

3. That Labrador retriever belongs to Chris and Jason. It won Best of Breed.

_____

4. Elizabeth and Matt each had a cocker spaniel. Those dogs were playful.

_____

5. Allison and Nicole each brought a beagle. The dogs chewed on their toys.

_____

13. Appositives

An **appositive** is a word that follows a noun. It renames the noun or explains its meaning. An **appositive phrase** is an appositive and its modifiers. A **nonrestrictive** appositive or appositive phrase is not essential to the meaning of the sentence. It is set off by commas. A **restrictive** appositive or appositive phrase is necessary to the meaning of a sentence. It is not set off by commas.

NONRESTRICTIVE **The American flag, <u>a symbol of our country</u>, is red, white, and blue.**
(The appositive is not necessary to know what color the flag is.)

RESTRICTIVE **The seamstress <u>Betsy Ross</u> is said to have made the first flag.**
(The appositive is necessary to know who the seamstress was.)

Circle each noun used as an appositive. Underline the noun(s) it renames or describes. On the line write **N** if the appositive is nonrestrictive or **R** if it is restrictive.

_N_ 1. The <u>Continental Congress</u>, a (group) of American patriots, played a key role in America's fight for independence.

_R_ 2. The Philadelphia <u>patriot</u> (Thomas Paine) wrote *Common Sense*.

_R_ 3. The Boston <u>politician</u> (Samuel Adams) opposed the British tax on tea.

_____ 4. Thomas Jefferson, a patriot from Virginia, wrote much of the Declaration of Independence.

_____ 5. John Hancock, the president of the Continental Congress, was the first signer of the Declaration of Independence.

_____ 6. The printer and inventor Benjamin Franklin also signed the document.

_____ 7. George III, the king of England, sent troops to the colonies.

_____ 8. The Battle of Lexington, the first armed fight of the American Revolution, took place on April 19, 1775.

_____ 9. George Washington, the first president of the United States, had commanded an army during the Revolutionary War.

_____ 10. The Polish officer Casimir Pulaski fought at the Battle of Brandywine.

_____ 11. The French aristocrat the Marquis de Lafayette also traveled to America to help the colonists.

_____ 12. The silversmith Paul Revere warned the people that British troops were going to attack soon.

_____ 13. The Redcoats, the British soldiers, could not defeat the colonists.

_____ 14. The British leader General Cornwallis lost several battles.

_____ 15. Yorktown, the last important battle of the war, was won by the Americans.

14. More Appositives

A subject, a subject complement, a direct object, an indirect object, or an object of a preposition can have an appositive.

Thomas Jefferson, a lawyer, held many public offices.
Jefferson became minister to France, the successor of Benjamin Franklin.
He designed his own home, Monticello.
The Continental Congress gave Thomas Jefferson, a good writer, the job of drafting a declaration of independence.
I am reading about Thomas Jefferson, our third president.

Underline each appositive. Circle the noun it explains.

1. Thomas Jefferson studied at the College of William and Mary, a school in Virginia.

2. He was appointed to the Second Continental Congress, the colonies' government, in 1775.

3. In 1776 Jefferson wrote the Declaration of Independence, a key document of American history.

4. The Declaration of Independence contained a long list of complaints about George III, the king of England.

5. In 1784 Jefferson agreed to succeed the U.S. ambassador to France, Benjamin Franklin.

6. Because Jefferson did not like to speak in public, as president he gave only two speeches, his inaugural addresses.

7. He even made the State of the Union address, the president's annual report to Congress, in writing.

8. Usually he did not meet in person with the cabinet, his political advisors.

9. Cabinet members sent him memos, summaries of their recommendations.

10. The Louisiana Purchase, the most important event in his presidency, took place in 1803.

11. Jefferson bought the territory from Napoleon, the leader of France.

12. Jefferson paid a low price, only $15 million dollars, for the entire territory.

13. Jefferson ordered his private secretary, Meriwether Lewis, to explore the new land.

14. After he left the presidency, Jefferson turned his attention to another interest, architecture.

15. Jefferson designed two new projects, the campus of the University of Virginia and a house in Bedford, Virginia.

Name _____

15. Words Used as Nouns and as Verbs

A noun is a naming word. A verb expresses action or being.
Many words can be used both as nouns and as verbs.

> NOUN
> **The study of planets reveals surprising facts.**
>
> VERB
> **Scientists study the planets.**

A. Above each *italicized* word write **N** if
the word is a noun or **V** if it is a verb.

1. The *rings* of Saturn are beautiful.

2. What material actually *rings* the planet?

3. Pieces of ice *form* the rings.

4. Some pieces are tiny ice particles, while others *reach* the size of icebergs.

5. In 1655 a Dutch astronomer first saw these round *forms* around Saturn.

6. Whenever possible, space probes *photograph* the rings up close.

7. Space probes can get close *views* of planets.

8. With telescopes, scientists could *view* only a few of Saturn's rings.

9. The *photographs* showed many rings around Saturn.

10. Space probes' photographs were a *surprise* to scientists.

11. What could *cause* Saturn's rings?

12. The *cause* may have been an explosion of one of Saturn's moons.

13. Forces slowly *pull* the ice in the rings down toward Saturn.

14. The *pull* of gravity is one of these forces.

15. New discoveries about planets may *surprise* scientists—and us—in the future.

B. Use each word in a sentence as a noun or a verb. The part of speech is indicated.

1. study (noun) _____

2. surprise (verb) _____

3. photograph (noun) _____

4. cause (verb) _____

5. view (noun) _____

16. Words Used as Nouns and as Adjectives

> A noun is a naming word. An adjective describes a noun. Some words can
> be used as nouns and as adjectives.
>
> | NOUN | ADJECTIVE | NOUN MODIFIED |
> |------|-----------|----------------|
> | **A bat is a mammal.** | **Large bat** | colonies are found in caves. |

Above each *italicized* word, write **A** if it is used as an adjective or
N if it is used as a noun.

1. Many people are scared of bats, but bats do a great deal of *good*.

2. For example, bats eat *insect* pests.

3. In one hour a bat can eat between 600 and 1,000 *insects*.

4. Therefore, bats are *good* for humans because they eliminate harmful insects.

5. They are also important to some *plants*.

6. Many *plant* species depend on bats for pollination.

7. Bats often live in a *cave*.

8. Bats may sleep in large groups, hanging from the *cave* ceiling.

9. Some bats spend the *winter* months in caves.

10. These bats sleep, or hibernate, during the *winter*.

11. Bats are primarily *night* animals.

12. They look for food during the *night* and sleep during the day.

13. Bats use *sound* to guide their movements.

14. The bats' *sound* emissions return to them as echoes, which enable the bats to detect objects ahead.

15. The bones in a bat's wing are similar to the bones in a human *finger*.

16. But the bat's *finger* bones are quite long.

17. Bats' large wings are covered with *membranes*.

18. The *membrane* structures of the wings allow bats to scoop insects in flight.

19. *Migration* for the winter is characteristic of some bats, as it is for birds.

20. Some of these *migration* flights take the bats from Mexico to the United States.

Name _____

18. Personal Pronouns

A **pronoun** is a word that is used in place of a noun. A **personal pronoun** changes form to show who is speaking (first person); who is being spoken to (second person); or who, what, or where is being spoken about (third person). The first person personal pronouns are *I, me, mine, we, us* and *ours;* the second person pronouns are *you* and *yours;* and the third person pronouns are *he, she, it, him, her, his, hers, its, they, them* and *theirs.*

FIRST PERSON

I am reading a book about Angelina Grimké.

SECOND PERSON

Do you know who she is?

THIRD PERSON

She crusaded against slavery before the Civil War.

Underline each personal pronoun. Above each pronoun write what person it shows—**1** for first person, **2** for second person, and **3** for third person.

ANGELINA

1. I learned about Angelina and Sarah Grimké; they were crusaders against slavery.

2. Slavery seemed terrible to them, and so they wanted to help end it.

3. The sisters wrote articles about slavery and published them in newspapers and magazines.

4. They told Southern women, "You should talk to your husbands and friends about slavery. Tell them that you think it is wrong."

SARAH

5. I think that we owe a great deal to people like Sarah and Angelina Grimké because they helped us in the fight for human rights.

Angelina and Sarah Grimké fought for the rights of others. Give an example of something you can do to help others in their struggle for human rights.

19. Number and Gender of Pronouns

A pronoun is **singular** when it refers to one person, place, or thing.
Tom sent an **e-mail** to his **mother**.
He sent **it** to **her**.

A pronoun is **plural** when it refers to more than one person, place, or thing.
Tonya and Maria brought some **cookies**.
They brought **them**.

A **third person singular pronoun** can be masculine, feminine, or neuter.
MASCULINE   FEMININE   NEUTER
He helped **her** prepare supper. I helped eat **it**.

A. Underline the personal pronoun(s) in each sentence.
Above each write **S** if it is singular or **P** if it is plural.

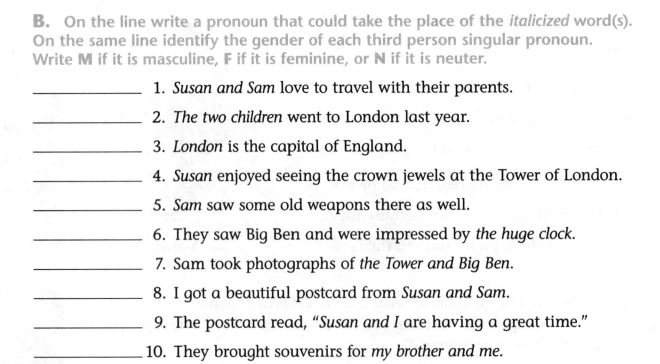

1. My brother and I love to travel.

2. Last year we took a trip to London.

3. It is a beautiful and historic city.

4. My brother went to see the changing of the guard, and he took a picture of the colorful ceremony.

5. We bought fish and chips every day and ate them for lunch.

B. On the line write a pronoun that could take the place of the *italicized* word(s). On the same line identify the gender of each third person singular pronoun. Write **M** if it is masculine, **F** if it is feminine, or **N** if it is neuter.

_____ 1. *Susan and Sam* love to travel with their parents.

_____ 2. *The two children* went to London last year.

_____ 3. *London* is the capital of England.

_____ 4. *Susan* enjoyed seeing the crown jewels at the Tower of London.

_____ 5. *Sam* saw some old weapons there as well.

_____ 6. They saw Big Ben and were impressed by *the huge clock*.

_____ 7. Sam took photographs of *the Tower and Big Ben*.

_____ 8. I got a beautiful postcard from *Susan and Sam*.

_____ 9. The postcard read, "*Susan and I* are having a great time."

_____ 10. They brought souvenirs for *my brother and me*.

20. Agreement of Pronouns and Antecedents

The noun to which a pronoun refers is its **antecedent**. The pronoun must agree in person and number with the noun it replaces. A third person singular pronoun must also agree with its antecedent in gender.

> <u>Mohandas Karamchand Gandhi</u> was born in India in 1869; <u>he</u> became an international figure for freedom.
>
> <u>India</u> is in Asia, but <u>it</u> was ruled by the British.

A. Underline the pronoun that goes with each *italicized* antecedent.

1. The people of India were not happy with British *rule* and wanted it to end.

2. Gandhi had read the writings of *Henry David Thoreau* and had learned about civil disobedience from him.

3. Gandhi was an example for the Indian *people,* and he taught them nonviolent ways to oppose the British authorities.

4. When *Gandhi* spoke about independence, people cheered him.

5. *Gandhi* asked Indians to stop wearing clothes made in England, and he encouraged them to set up their own clothing industry.

B. Complete each sentence with a pronoun that refers to the *italicized* antecedent.

1. As *Gandhi* worked for independence, _____ often fasted.

2. He used fasting to show *people* that _____ needed to be nonviolent.

3. The Indian people loved *Gandhi* and called _____ Mahatma, which means "great soul."

4. In 1947 the British left *India,* and _____ became independent.

5. In 1948 *Gandhi* was murdered by a fanatic while _____ was on his way to a prayer meeting.

Mohandas K. Gandhi used only peaceful means to achieve his goals. Give an example of some peaceful means you can use to deal with people who think differently than you do.

21. Intensive Pronouns and Reflexive Pronouns

> Reflexive pronouns and intensive pronouns end in *-self* or *-selves*. A **reflexive pronoun** is used as a direct object, an indirect object, or the object of a preposition. A reflexive pronoun usually refers back to the subject. An **intensive pronoun** is used to emphasize the preceding noun or pronoun; it is not essential to the sentence.
>
> REFLEXIVE   **Trent sent himself a copy of the message.**
> **Many inventors do not work by themselves.**
>
> INTENSIVE   **I myself made the grilled cheese sandwich.**
> **I made the grilled cheese sandwich myself.**

A. Underline each reflexive pronoun. Circle each intensive pronoun.

1. Alexander Graham Bell invented the telephone, but he did not do all the work by himself.

2. Bell had the help of Thomas Watson. Watson himself built the prototype phones from Bell's designs.

3. Bell and Watson did all the testing of the instruments by themselves.

4. Bell earned himself the title of inventor of the phone with the first voice transmission in 1876.

5. Bell's wife herself, Mabel Hubbard Bell, was interested in science.

6. She and her husband built themselves a large home in Canada where they could conduct their research.

7. Mabel Bell was deaf, but she set high goals for herself.

8. She was interested in developing airplanes and other flying machines, though she herself was never able to fly in one.

9. Alexander Graham Bell himself was responsible for new teaching methods and inventions to help the deaf.

10. We should remind ourselves of all the people like Bell who helped people have better lives.

B. Complete each sentence with the correct reflexive pronoun.

1. I cut _____ while I was chopping onions.

2. Cats clean and groom _____ with their tongues.

3. We bought _____ some popcorn to eat during the movie.

4. Oscar, you must do the project for the science fair by _____.

5. Marybeth taught _____ the rules of chess.

22. Pronouns as Subjects

> A personal pronoun can be used as the subject of a sentence.
> The **subject pronouns** are *I, we, you, he, she, it,* and *they.*
>
> **I saw the White House on a news report last night.**
> **It is a really beautiful building.**

Circle the correct pronoun in parentheses.

1. Jill, Mark, and (I me) prepared a report on Washington, D.C.

2. (We Us) did research on the Internet and at the library.

3. Pierre L'Enfant designed the city. (Him He) was from France.

4. The city was named for George Washington.
   (He Him) hired L'Enfant to design it.

5. The White House is the home of the president.
   (It They) has been the home of every
   American president since John Adams.

6. Thomas Jefferson entered the contest for the design of
   the White House. (Him He) did not win, however.

7. Dolley Madison was the wife of President James Madison. (She Her)
   rescued papers from the White House before the British burned it in 1814.

8. First Lady Jacqueline Kennedy made important contributions to the White House.
   (She Her) redecorated it with antiques and historic paintings.

9. The Washington Monument honors the country's first president.
   (It They) was opened to the public in 1885.

10. Members of the House of Representatives meet in the Capitol. The senators
    and (they them) form the legislative branch of the government.

11. The John F. Kennedy Center for the Performing Arts is in Washington, D.C.
    (They It) contains various theaters for concerts, drama, and opera.

12. (You Me) can visit many historical sites in Washington, D.C., including the
    White House, the Capitol, and the Smithsonian Institution.

13. My family and (I me) visited Washington, D.C., last spring.

14. (It She) is a really beautiful city, espcially during Cherry Blossom Festival.

15. What do (you me) want to see when you visit Washington, D.C.?

Name _____

23. Pronouns as Subject Complements

A subject complement follows a linking verb and refers to the same person, place, or thing as the subject. The most common linking verbs are forms of the verb *be* (*is, are, was, were,* and so on). A **subject pronoun** can be used as a subject complement.

The editor of the school paper is <u>she</u>.

It is <u>I</u> who washed all the dishes.

A. Circle the correct pronoun in parentheses.

1. The assistant editors are Kristen and (she her).

2. It was (her she) who wrote the lead story in this issue of the paper.

3. It was (he him) who drew the cartoon that illustrated the story.

4. The photographers for the paper are Jason and (they them).

5. The page designers are Allison and (me I).

6. The English teachers were (they them) who suggested this special edition.

7. Principal Sharon Kent was (she her) who gave the go-ahead.

8. She told Ernesto that the person in charge would be (he him).

9. We knew that neither Charlie nor Phil would be (him he)—the copyboy.

10. The people writing the stories were (them they), the regular staff members.

11. Martha and Sue, as usual, would be (them they) who wrote the fashion stories.

12. I asked whether the entertainment editors could be (us we)—Katrina, Ann, and I.

13. Ernesto said that since I was already doing page design, the editors would probably be (they them).

14. When this special issue comes out, the students getting the first copies will be (us we) who did all the work.

15. The next group to receive copies will most likely be (they them) who gave their support and guidance.

B. Complete each sentence with a personal pronoun. Vary your choices.

1. The first ones to cross the finish line were _____.

2. The student who will sing onstage is _____.

3. Are you sure the coach was _____ in the gym?

4. The winning designers were _____ who were on television.

5. Was the person in the skeleton costume _____?

FINISH

3 5 . 2 8 . 5 9

24. Pronouns as Direct Objects

> A personal pronoun can be used as the direct object of a verb.
> The **object pronouns** are *me, us, you, him, her, it,* and *them.*
>
> **Julius Caesar was a ruler of Rome.**
> **His enemies killed <u>him</u> in 44 BC.**

A. Circle the correct pronoun in parentheses.

1. Julius Caesar was a leader in the Roman army.
   He joined (it him) as a young man.

2. He met a woman, Calpurnia, from a wealthy
   family and married (she her) in 59 BC.

3. The Romans had selected (he him) for
   public office 16 years earlier.

4. Caesar went to Gaul—what is now France—and conquered (it them).

5. Caesar had enemies in Rome. He defeated (they them) in 45 BC
   and took over the government.

6. As a ruler, Caesar reformed the calendar. We still use (them it)
   in a modified version today.

7. The Romans honored (he him) by naming July after him.

8. His stories about his battles survive, and people still read (them they).

9. Caesar's enemies killed (he him) on March 15, 44 BC.

10. Upon his death, Antony and Octavian succeeded (him he).

B. Use a personal pronoun to replace the word(s) in parentheses.

1. Cleopatra ruled _____ (Egypt) from 51 to 30 BC.

2. Five years after becoming queen, Cleopatra met _____ (Antony).

3. He fell in love with Cleopatra, and he married _____ (Cleopatra).

4. The couple wanted more power, and this angered _____ (the Romans).

5. Octavian went to Egypt and defeated Antony and _____ (Cleopatra).
   The couple killed themselves.

25. Pronouns as Indirect Objects

> An object pronoun can be used as the **indirect object** in a sentence. The indirect object tells *to whom, for whom, to what,* or *for what* something is done.
>
> **The coach gave us our instructions.**

A. Circle the indirect object in each sentence.

1. Tom sent me an invitation to his birthday party.

2. I bought him a present.

3. His mom offered us cake and ice cream.

4. We gave her our thanks.

5. Several guests sang him the birthday song.

6. He awarded them prizes.

7. His dad told us some funny stories.

8. We paid him many compliments.

9. Tom's mother brought us our coats.

10. I'll send her a thank-you note tomorrow.

B. Complete each sentence with the correct form of the pronoun indicated in parentheses.

1. I sent _____ a letter of complaint. *(second, singular)*

2. Please give _____ an answer. *(first, singular)*

3. The reporter asked _____ a question. *(third, singular, feminine)*

4. The government denied _____ their rights. *(third, plural)*

5. His mother made _____ a sandwich. *(third, singular, masculine)*

6. The teacher told _____ a story. *(first, plural)*

7. The incident taught _____ a lesson. *(third, singular, feminine)*

8. I think you owe _____ an apology. *(first, singular)*

9. We found _____ a new home. *(third, singular, neuter)*

10. His project earned _____ a good grade. *(third, singular, masculine)*

26. Pronouns as Objects of Prepositions

> An object pronoun can be used as the object of a preposition.
>
> **The teacher wanted to talk to __me__ about my science fair project.**

A. Circle the correct pronoun in parentheses.

1. Yesterday the coach read some basic basketball rules to (we us).

2. Paul told the joke to Luisa and (I me).

3. Mrs. Russo lives near (us we).

4. Is this orange juice for Maggie and (he him)?

5. The decorations for the party were made by (them they).

6. We sat in the theater balcony, and below (we us) was the entire choral group.

7. Sarah's mother forgot to give the message to (her she).

8. Frank spotted his best friend and quickly walked toward (him he).

9. Everybody has gone home except Chris and (he him).

10. I went to the Grand Canyon last fall and took pictures of (it she).

B. Write the correct object form of the pronoun in parentheses to complete each sentence.

1. I got a long e-mail from _____ (she).

2. Vassily stood near _____ (I) in the cafeteria line.

3. I have told this story about Mom and _____ (they) before.

4. We can't leave for the mall without _____ (she).

5. My brother Carlos loves fixing up his car. Last weekend he bought some new wheel covers for _____ (it).

6. Lee wants to work on the science project with Rita and _____ (I).

7. Everyone except _____ (he) is in school today.

8. Here is an apple for _____ (you).

9. Bea and Ann divided the cookies among the three of _____ (we).

10. He called on everyone in class except Ryan and _____ (she).

27. Possessive Pronouns

> A **possessive pronoun** shows possession or ownership. A possessive pronoun stands by itself; it does not modify a noun. A possessive pronoun does not have an apostrophe. The possessive pronouns are *mine, yours, his, hers, its, ours,* and *theirs.*
>
> **That history book is <u>mine</u>.**   <u>**Yours**</u> **is in your backpack.**

A. Underline the possessive pronoun(s) in each sentence.

1. That new skateboard is hers.

2. Ours is much larger, and yours is much smaller.

3. Mine is purple and green.

4. Those two skateboards must be theirs.

5. His is under the bed.

6. I can't find my bat. Please let me use yours.

7. This bat isn't mine. I think it's his.

8. Excuse me. Is this glove yours?

9. I left mine in the gym at school.

10. Luke lost a glove. This glove must be his.

B. Write on the line the possessive pronoun related to the personal pronoun in parentheses.

1. The green pencil is _____ (she).

2. The idea for the project was _____ (they).

3. Please put your bicycle over there beside _____ (we).

4. The last house on the street is _____ (he).

5. No, those apples are not _____ (I).

6. Are these books _____ (you)?

7. _____ (I) has been missing for a week.

8. Find _____ (you) and then find _____ (she).

9. The prize-winning project was _____ (she).

10. Is this jacket _____ (he) or _____ (she)?

Pronouns

28. Possessive Adjectives

A **possessive adjective** expresses possession or ownership. A possessive adjective modifies a noun. The possessive adjectives are *my, our, your, his, her, its,* and *their.*

I got <u>my</u> tetanus shot yesterday.

A. Underline the possessive adjective in each sentence.

1. My report is about vaccines.

2. Vaccines protect our bodies from many diseases.

3. Edward Jenner invented the first vaccine in 1798, and his work had important results.

4. His vaccine protected people against smallpox.

5. He studied a minor disease, cowpox, and noticed its effects on people.

6. After people had suffered from cowpox, their bodies were able to fight off smallpox.

7. Jenner had an idea: his idea was to inject people with cowpox bacteria.

8. Jenner's experiments were a success in the fight against smallpox, and their results led to the development of other vaccines.

9. Edna told me that she had done her report on vaccines too.

10. We found, however, that our reports focused on different scientists.

B. Write the correct form of the possessive adjective on the line. Use the adjective related to the pronoun in parentheses.

1. People need to do many things to protect _____ (they) health.

2. We need to make sure that we get all _____ (we) vaccinations.

3. When you receive a vaccine, it helps _____ (you) body create antibodies to fight a disease.

4. Sometimes a person's body can create _____ (it) own antibodies.

5. The vaccines fight such dangerous diseases as polio, diphtheria, and tetanus. Doctors know that these diseases and _____ (they) effects can be serious.

29. Possessive Adjectives and Contractions

A possessive adjective expresses possession or ownership. A possessive adjective does not have an apostrophe. A **contraction** generally is formed by joining a personal pronoun and a verb. An apostrophe (') replaces the missing letter or letters.

POSSESSIVE ADJECTIVE **Your report is on the fall of the Berlin Wall.**

CONTRACTION **You're (= You are) supposed to give the report next week.**

A. Write **P** over the underlined word if it is a possessive adjective. Write **C** if it is a contraction.

1. The students studied about the Berlin Wall in <u>their</u> social studies class.

2. <u>Its</u> fall on November 9, 1989, marked communism's end in Germany.

3. <u>It's</u> been interesting to study about the reuniting of East Germany and West Germany.

4. <u>They're</u> now a single country.

5. What is <u>your</u> opinion about the fall of the Berlin Wall?

B. Circle the correct word in parentheses.

1. The people of Poland had many of the same problems as the people of East Germany. From 1945 (their they're) government was Communist.

2. (They're Their) no longer under Communist rule.

3. (Their They're) transition to democracy began in 1980.

4. In that year workers formed (their they're) opposition trade union, Solidarity.

5. (Its It's) leader was Lech Walesa.

6. Communists opposed the union, and (its it's) existence was banned.

7. People supported the union, and (their they're) support kept it alive.

8. In 1989 Poland had an economic crisis. (It's Its) Communist leaders then decided to allow Solidarity to participate in elections.

9. Solidarity won many seats in the Polish congress; it reformed Poland's economy and gave back to the people (their they're) freedoms.

10. The Polish people are glad that (they're their) free to form their own government.

30. More Contractions

> A personal pronoun and a verb can be joined to form a contraction. In a contraction an apostrophe replaces the missing letter or letters.
>
> **I'm** (= I am) **writing a report on Morocco.**
> **We've** (= We have) **never visited Morocco.**

A. Underline the contraction in each item. Write the pronoun and the verb that make up the contraction in the appropriate columns.

	PRONOUN	VERB

1. Morocco is a fascinating country. It's located in northwest Africa. _____ _____

2. The head of the government is a king. He's named Muhammad VI. _____ _____

3. He's been king since 1999. _____ _____

4. Morocco has many mountains. They're among the tallest mountains in northern Africa. _____ _____

5. Many Moroccans have moved to large cities. They've created a severe housing crisis in cities such as Casablanca and Fez. _____ _____

6. Morocco was colonized by Spain and France. It's been independent since 1956. _____ _____

7. Moroccans speak French and Arabic. They're mostly employed in agricultural jobs. _____ _____

8. The capital is Rabat. It's a beautiful modern city located on the Atlantic Ocean. _____ _____

9. I've never been to Morocco. _____ _____

10. But we're going to visit Morocco next year. _____ _____

B. Complete each sentence with the correct contraction. Use the pronoun and verb at the left.

He is   1. Morocco's ruler is named Muhammad VI. _____ the King of Morocco.

It is   2. _____ on the Atlantic Ocean and the Mediterranean Sea.

It has   3. _____ been ruled by Spain and France.

They are   4. The people are religious. _____ mostly Muslims.

I am   5. _____ going to write a report on Morocco for school.

31. Demonstrative Pronouns

Demonstrative pronouns are used to point out things, places, and people. Use *this* and *these* to point out things that are near. Use *that* and *those* to point out things that are farther away. *This* and *that* are singular. *These* and *those* are plural.

This is my sweater.
These are my hiking boots.

That is my water bottle.
Those are my jeans.

A. Circle the demonstrative pronoun. In Column 1 write **N** for near or **F** for far. In Column 2 write **S** for singular or **P** for plural.

	COLUMN 1	COLUMN 2
1. These are the things we need for our camping trip.	_____	_____
2. That is the tent we'll take.	_____	_____
3. Whose sunglasses are these?	_____	_____
4. This is good bug repellant.	_____	_____
5. That is Dad's flashlight.	_____	_____
6. Those are the wrong batteries.	_____	_____
7. We need candles. Please pack these.	_____	_____
8. Whose guidebook is this?	_____	_____
9. Is that your sleeping bag?	_____	_____
10. Are those the inflatable pillows?	_____	_____

B. Complete each sentence with a demonstrative pronoun. Use the directions in parentheses.

1. Are _____ the supplies for the art project? (far)

2. _____ are not the correct markers. (near)

3. Is _____ your canvas? (near)

4. _____ are my watercolors. (near)

5. _____ is a box of felt scraps. (far)

6. Whose wooden pegs are _____? (far)

7. _____ is the glue gun I need. (near)

8. Can you drill a hole with _____? (far)

9. I need some washers. Please hand me _____. (far)

10. Is _____ the tool you need? (near)

Pronouns

32. Interrogative Pronouns

An **interrogative pronoun** is used to ask a question. The interrogative
pronouns are *who, whom, which, what,* and *whose.*
  What is the name of the spacecraft that flew to Mars?

The interrogative pronoun *who* is used when the pronoun refers to a person
and when it is the subject of a question.
  Who was the first person to walk on the Moon?

The interrogative pronoun *whom* is used when the pronoun refers to a
person and when it is the direct object or the indirect object of a verb
or the object of a preposition.
  **Whom did the United States have as its first female commander
  of a space flight?**

A. Underline the interrogative pronoun in each sentence.
Write whether it refers to a person or a thing.

_____ 1. Who were the first Americans to land on the Moon?

_____ 2. What did the spacecraft use as fuel?

_____ 3. Which of the astronauts walked on the Moon first?

_____ 4. Who called the astronauts while they were on the Moon?

_____ 5. What did the astronauts bring back from the Moon?

B. Complete each sentence with *which, what,* or *whose.*

1. _____ of the planets did American spacecraft visit first, Mars or Venus?

2. _____ was the nationality of the first person to travel in space?

3. _____ was the promise that the United States would
   explore the Moon within a decade?

4. _____ is a cosmonaut?

5. _____ of these countries was the first to launch
   a rocket into space, the Soviet Union or the United States?

C. Complete each sentence with *who* or *whom.*

1. _____ is Neil Armstrong?

2. _____ was the first Russian to travel in space?

3. To _____ did the astronauts send their messages
   from the Moon?

4. _____ did you discuss in your report, Neil Armstrong or John Glenn?

5. _____ was the captain of the latest *Discovery* flight?

33. Indefinite Pronouns

An **indefinite pronoun** refers to any or all of a group of persons, places, or things. Among the indefinite pronouns are *anybody, anyone, anything, everybody, everyone, everything, nobody, no one, nothing, somebody, someone, something, both, few, each, either, many, neither, several, all,* and *some.*

We're studying European nations. Many are on the Mediterranean.

Each of the countries on the Mediterranean uses it for recreation.

A. Underline the indefinite pronoun(s) in each sentence.

1. Almost everybody in Italy speaks Italian, and almost everyone in Spain speaks Spanish.

2. These languages are among several that are based on Latin.

3. In both of the countries, people enjoy religious freedom.

4. Many of the cities have beautiful churches and museums.

5. The people are very friendly. If you get lost, anybody will help you.

6. Someone mentioned that Spain covers a larger area than Italy does.

7. Italy and Spain have one great similarity: each is located on a peninsula.

8. Neither is as large as Texas.

9. Each has a rich cultural heritage.

10. Do you want to visit either of these countries?

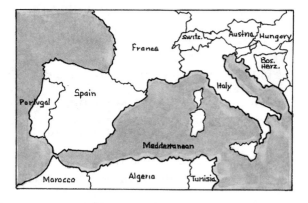

B. Complete each sentence with an indefinite pronoun.

1. _____ of the countries are democracies.

2. _____ are on the Mediterranean.

3. Do you know _____ from Spain or Italy?

4. _____ of my grandparents came from these countries.

5. What is the most interesting fact you know about _____ of these countries?

Name _____

34. Verbs with Indefinite Pronouns

Pronouns

A. On the line write **S** if the *italicized* pronoun is singular or **P** if it is plural. Circle the correct verb.

_____ 1. *Everyone* (admires admire) the beauty of gold and silver.

_____ 2. *Both* (has have) been highly valued for hundreds of years.

_____ 3. *Neither* (is are) found in great abundance on the earth.

_____ 4. *Both* of them (is are) precious metals.

_____ 5. *Each* (last lasts) a long time, but silver tends to turn black.

_____ 6. *Many* of the earth's metals (shine shines), and both gold and silver have a luster.

_____ 7. *Either* (is are) frequently used in jewelry designs.

_____ 8. *Some* of the objects in ancient tombs (is are) gold jewelry.

_____ 9. *Many* of the pieces of jewelry (is are) beautiful.

_____ 10. *Nobody* (fails fail) to admire the magnificent gold mask of the Egyptian king Tut.

B. Complete the sentences with *was* or *were.*

1. Two great gold rushes occurred in United States history.
   Both _____ during the 19th century.

2. Each _____ to a different location, California and Alaska.

3. Many of the miners _____ immigrants from Europe and Asia.

4. Everyone _____ interested in getting rich.

5. However, very few _____ lucky enough to find gold.

35. Indefinite Pronouns and Double Negatives

The indefinite pronouns *nothing, no one,* and *nobody* are negatives. When a sentence contains a negative word such as *never* or *not,* do not use a negative pronoun. Instead, use *anything, anyone,* or *anybody.*

Kevin could <u>not</u> read <u>anything</u> on the chalkboard.

Kevin could read <u>nothing</u> on the chalkboard.

Circle the correct indefinite pronoun in parentheses.

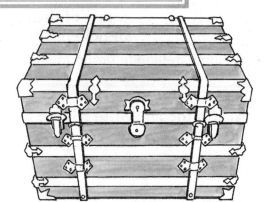

1. Tim didn't find (nothing anything) in the old trunk in the attic.

2. I'm sorry. There is (nothing anything) in the mailbox for you today.

3. (Anybody Nobody) spoke about the problem of air pollution.

4. I have never seen (no one anyone) as tall as Kevin Garnett!

5. Sydney broke his arm and can't carry (anything nothing).

6. (Nobody Anybody) wants to go out in this heavy downpour.

7. I found (anything nothing) in the parking lot except broken glass.

8. The winner was so excited that she couldn't say (nothing anything).

9. This week (nobody anybody) in our class arrived late to school.

10. Carmen hasn't eaten (anything nothing) since breakfast.

11. (Anybody Nobody) should have been in the park after dark.

12. I didn't tell the secret to (anybody nobody).

13. Our plan is foolproof! (Nothing Anything) can go wrong.

14. Doesn't (anybody nobody) know a good baseball Web site?

15. The detectives looked for clues, but they couldn't find (nothing anything).

16. The last math problem was so difficult that (nobody anybody) could solve it.

17. Bears live near this campground, so keep all your food in the car. Don't leave (anything nothing) in your tent.

18. I spent four hours at the mall, but I didn't buy (anything nothing).

19. There wasn't (anything nothing) in the refrigerator.

20. Accidents can happen to (anyone no one).

Pronouns

37. Descriptive Adjectives

Adjectives describe nouns. Descriptive adjectives can tell about age, size, shape, color, origin, or other qualities.

The large painting hung near the south entrance of the museum. Italian artists painted on wet plaster to create frescos.

A. Circle each descriptive adjective. Underline the noun it describes.

1. Throughout history, people have made pictures in different ways.
2. Early people painted on the walls of caves.
3. They used colorful pigments made from soil.
4. Egyptians boiled various plants to make dyes.
5. People in Asia made remarkable colors from clay.
6. European painters in the 1300s made paints from eggs.
7. Painters today often use acrylic paints.
8. Crayons made of wax and pigment come in bright colors.
9. Creative artists sometimes use crayons to draw pictures.
10. Sculptors sometimes make mammoth constructions out of metal.
11. They may also make collages of simple objects that they find.
12. Delicate drawings can be made with pen and ink.
13. Artists today do original work with videos.
14. They use computers to adjust digital photos.
15. Beautiful art can be found almost anywhere.

B. Write an adjective to describe each noun.

1. _____ sunset
2. _____ field
3. _____ puppy
4. _____ boat
5. _____ artist
6. _____ painting
7. _____ pizza
8. _____ skateboard
9. _____ report
10. _____ computer

38. More Descriptive Adjectives

Descriptive adjectives tell about characteristics such as age, size, shape, color, taste, or origin.

In the <u>old</u> basket were <u>large</u>, <u>round</u>, <u>red</u> apples.

A. Put each adjective in the appropriate column. Then add two adjectives of your own to each column.

circular	large	Danish	new	pink
purple	square	young	tiny	Thai

AGE	SIZE	SHAPE	COLOR	ORIGIN
_____	_____	_____	_____	_____
_____	_____	_____	_____	_____
_____	_____	_____	_____	_____
_____	_____	_____	_____	_____

B. Complete each sentence with the correct adjective. Use the clue in parentheses for help. Use each adjective once.

excellent	green	Italian	old	popular
delicious	healthful	large	orange	sweet

1. *Zucchini* is an _____ (origin) word that means "little squash."

2. Zucchini are _____ (quality) vegetables that are good for everyone.

3. Because zucchini are low in calories, they are an _____ (quality) choice for dieters.

4. Cooks choose zucchini with shiny, _____ (color) skins.

5. Zucchini have a delicate, almost _____ (taste) flavor.

6. Small zucchini are usually less bland than _____ (size) ones.

7. People make _____ (taste) salads with raw zucchini.

8. It is an _____ (age) custom in Italy to eat zucchini cooked with eggplant, tomatoes, and peppers.

9. Another _____ (quality) use of zucchini is in zucchini bread.

10. The bright _____ (color) and yellow zucchini flowers are also edible.

39. Definite and Indefinite Articles

> *A*, *an*, and *the* are a type of adjective that points out nouns. They are called **articles**. *The* is a **definite article**. *A* and *an* are **indefinite articles**.
> The article *an* is used before a vowel sound.
> The article *a* is used before a consonant sound.
>
> **The tourists went to <u>an</u> island for <u>a</u> vacation.**

A. Write the correct indefinite article before each word.

1. _____ lieutenant
2. _____ eclipse
3. _____ albatross
4. _____ chauffeur
5. _____ hexagon

6. _____ application
7. _____ dinosaur
8. _____ musician
9. _____ orphan
10. _____ rainbow

11. _____ elephant
12. _____ folktale
13. _____ egg
14. _____ accident
15. _____ cellular phone

B. Complete each sentence with definite or indefinite articles as indicated.

1. _____ *(definite)* South Pacific has many islands.

2. It is _____ *(indefinite)* part of _____ *(definite)* world that has more water than land.

3. Volcanoes and atolls formed _____ *(definite)* islands of the South Pacific.

4. _____ *(definite)* animals of _____ *(definite)* islands include bats and lizards.

5. Sometimes _____ *(indefinite)* typhoon strikes _____ *(definite)* islands.

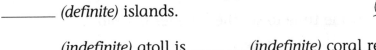
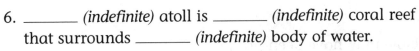

6. _____ *(indefinite)* atoll is _____ *(indefinite)* coral reef that surrounds _____ *(indefinite)* body of water.

7. _____ *(definite)* Great Barrier Reef, _____ *(indefinite)* wall of coral, is in Australia.

8. On _____ *(indefinite)* reef there is _____ *(indefinite)* abundance of wildlife.

9. You might see _____ *(indefinite)* shark hiding in _____ *(definite)* shadows.

10. Would you like to visit _____ *(indefinite)* island in _____ *(definite)* South Pacific?

40. Numerical Adjectives

A **numerical adjective** indicates an exact number. It may refer to the number of persons or things, or it may refer to an arrangement of things in numerical order. Numerical adjectives may be written as numerals or as words.

Gutenberg was the <u>first</u> person to use moveable type to print a book.

About <u>51</u> copies of the Bible he printed are known to exist today.

Underline each numerical adjective.
Circle the noun it modifies.

1. Johann Gutenberg lived in Germany during the fifteenth century.

2. At that time books were copied by hand, and it sometimes took a scribe two years or more to copy a book.

3. Gutenberg, a skilled inventor and metal worker, spent twenty years on his printing experiments.

4. He used small pieces of metal, each with one letter on it.

5. His set of type had 290 different characters: letters, punctuation marks, and joined letters required by medieval Latin.

6. He created pages with the type and then printed one page at a time on a printing press made from an old wine press.

7. Soon after Gutenberg perfected his press, he had a disagreement with a partner and paid him 2,025 guilders, a great deal of money at that time.

8. Gutenberg printed two books, a Bible and another religious work.

9. This Bible had forty-two lines of type on each page.

10. Each page had about 2,500 characters.

11. Six typesetters worked at the same time to set the type for the Bible.

12. It was printed in three volumes.

13. About 200 copies of the Bible may have been printed.

14. Gutenberg's system of typesetting was so good that it was used without significant change until the twentieth century.

15. His method of printing survived for more than 400 years!

Johann Gutenberg worked patiently for twenty years on his printing experiments. Give an example of a situation in which you needed patience to achieve your goal.

Adjectives

41. Adjectives as Subject Complements

An adjective that follows a linking verb and completes the meaning of a sentence is called a **subject complement**. It describes or explains the subject.

SUBJECT (NOUN)   SUBJECT COMPLEMENT (ADJECTIVE)
Switzerland   is   **mountainous.**

Underline each subject complement. Circle the noun it describes.

1. Switzerland is small.

2. The country is multilingual: people speak German, French, and Italian.

3. Switzerland has been neutral during wars.

4. The country's government is democratic.

5. Switzerland is wealthy.

6. The people are industrious and hardworking.

7. Swiss banks have long been famous around the world.

8. Industrial production is high.

9. Swiss products are excellent.

10. Swiss chocolate is delicious.

11. Swiss watches are famous.

12. The watches are extremely accurate.

13. Many Swiss watches are also expensive.

14. Swiss watchmakers have always been careful and precise in their work.

15. The weather is often rainy.

16. Winters are cold and snowy.

17. The weather can be foggy in the winter.

18. In winter, skiing conditions are excellent.

19. During winter months resorts are busy with skiers.

20. The Swiss countryside is beautiful.

42. Position of Adjectives

> An adjective can be used before a noun or following a linking verb as a subject complement.
>
> **Tidal waves are dangerous.**

A. Identify the position of each *italicized* adjective. Above the adjective write **BN** if it comes before the noun and **SC** if it is a subject complement.

1. In summer the climate of Florida is *hot*.

2. The weather is often *humid* too.

3. During these *hot* months the beaches are *crowded*.

4. In winter, temperatures remain *warm*.

5. Winter nights are usually *cool*.

6. Florida has thousands of miles of *sandy* beaches.

7. The *beautiful* beaches and *warm* climate attract tourists to Florida.

8. Tourism is *important* to Florida's economy.

9. Florida has *fabulous* restaurants with *excellent* seafood.

10. Vacations in Florida can be *wonderful*.

B. Underline each adjective that comes before a noun. Circle each adjective that follows a linking verb.

1. The United States is rich in natural resources.

2. Large rivers are useful for shipping.

3. Northern forests are valuable for wood.

4. Coal is a valuable resource that can't be renewed.

5. Fossil fuels will not be plentiful forever.

6. Fertile soils are rich in minerals.

7. Certain metals are vital to the economy.

8. American mines are large and productive.

9. Natural resources are important to everyone.

10. People should be careful to use them wisely.

43. Comparative and Superlative Adjectives

Most adjectives have three degrees of comparison: positive, comparative, and superlative. The **positive degree** describes a quality or a characteristic of a noun. The **comparative degree** is used to compare two items or two sets of items. It is formed by adding *-er* after the adjective or *more* or *less* before the adjective. The **superlative degree** is used to compare three or more items. It is formed by adding *-est* after the adjective or *most* or *least* before the adjective.

POSITIVE	Hydroelectric power, produced by flowing water, isn't very old.
COMPARATIVE	The steam engine is older than hydroelectric power.
SUPERLATIVE	Power from wind and water are among the oldest types of power.

A. Write the comparative and superlative degrees of each adjective.

1. sharp _____ _____

2. heavy _____ _____

3. large _____ _____

4. good _____ _____

5. cold _____ _____

6. expensive _____ _____

7. honest _____ _____

8. peaceful _____ _____

9. annoying _____ _____

10. dangerous _____ _____

B. On the line write **C** if the *italicized* adjective is in the comparative degree or **S** if it is in the superlative degree.

_____ 1. Water is one of our *most important* natural resources.

_____ 2. The hydroelectric-power process is *cleaner* than the coal-burning process.

_____ 3. Water pollution is one of the country's *biggest* problems.

_____ 4. Thirty years ago Lake Erie was one of the *most polluted* lakes in the country.

_____ 5. Today the water in Lake Erie is much *purer.*

44. More Comparative and Superlative Adjectives

> The comparative degree is used when two persons, places, or things are compared.
> **Hurricanes are stronger than tornadoes. They are more destructive too.**
>
> The superlative degree is used when more than two are compared.
> **What was the strongest hurricane in history? Was it most destructive?**

A. Circle the correct adjective form in each sentence.

1. Hurricanes are among the (dangerous   most dangerous) types of storms.

2. Hurricane Katrina, in 2005, was a (terrible   more terrible) hurricane;
   it caused more than $100 billion in damage.

3. In some ways, however, it wasn't the (worse   worst) hurricane in history.

4. Which hurricane was the (most destructive   more destructive) in history?

5. A 1900 hurricane was (deadlier   deadliest) than Katrina.

6. That hurricane in Galveston, Texas, resulted in the (higher   highest) death toll
   from a hurricane in the United States; about 8,000 people died.

7. No storm has been (worse   worst) in terms of loss of life.

8. After the storm the city of Galveston built a (large   largest) seawall.

9. The seawall is the (more elevated   most elevated) point of land on the island where
   Galveston is located.

10. The city is (safer   safest) from violent storms because of the seawall.

B. Complete each sentence with the correct form of the adjective.

1. The sinking of the *Titanic* was one of the _____
   (shocking) events in the 20th century.

2. It was also _____ (bad) than any
   other tragedy at sea; more than 1,500 people died.

3. When the *Titanic* was built in 1912, it was the
   _____ (big) passenger ship
   in the world.

4. It was also one of the _____
   (luxurious) ships.

5. Nowadays ships are _____ (safe)
   than the *Titanic* because they carry enough lifeboats for everyone aboard.

Adjectives

45. Little, Less, Least and Few, Fewer, Fewest

Count nouns name things that can be counted. They have plural forms. Use *few, fewer, fewest* to compare count nouns. **Noncount nouns** name things that cannot be counted. They do not have plural forms. Use *little, less, least* to compare noncount nouns.

Tom has a <u>few quarters</u>. Tom has very <u>little change</u>.
Tom has <u>fewer quarters</u> than   Tom has <u>less change</u> than Joe does.
Joe does.
Tom has the <u>fewest quarters</u>   Tom has the <u>least change</u> of all
of all the boys.   the boys.

A. Write *little* or *few* to complete each sentence.

1. Deserts get very _____ rain.

2. Only a _____ animals can live in a desert environment.

3. _____ vegetation grows in the desert.

4. _____ types of plants can survive the harsh conditions.

5. Many desert plants have very _____ leaves.

B. Write *less* or *fewer* to complete each sentence.

1. The carpenter had _____ hammers than screwdrivers.

2. He had _____ tools than the other workers had.

3. He made _____ progress than the others made.

4. He also gave the others _____ advice.

5. I think he made _____ money than anyone else.

C. Write *least* or *fewest* to complete each sentence.

1. My aunt has the _____ jewelry of the three women.

2. She owns the _____ rings of all.

3. She also has the _____ bracelets.

4. She puts the _____ importance on material things.

5. She has the _____ needs of anyone I know.

46. Demonstrative Adjectives

> A **demonstrative adjective** points out the thing it refers to.
> The demonstrative adjectives are *this, that, these* and *those.*
> *This* and *that* point out one person, place, or thing.
> *These* and *those* point out more than one person, place, or thing.
> *This* and *these* name persons, places, or things that are near.
> *That* and *those* name persons, places, or things that are far.
>
> **This rock is a special kind of rock—a fossil.**
> **That rock contains a rare mineral, gold.**
> **These rocks are made of quartz.**
> **Those rocks are nothing but gravel.**

A. Underline each demonstrative adjective.

1. That scientist is a geologist.

2. The formation of this planet is a geologist's field of study.

3. These scientists collect rock samples for study.

4. Fossilized plants and animals help these people reconstruct the past.

5. Fossils are important in this kind of work.

6. Dating those specimens provides useful information to scientists.

7. Many areas of science benefit from this knowledge.

8. That insect was preserved in fossilized tree sap.

9. The name of that fossil is amber.

10. Those plants and animals preserved as fossils lived millions of years ago.

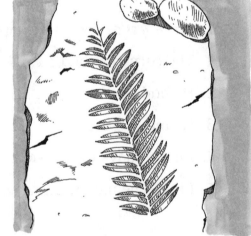

B. Complete each sentence with a demonstrative adjective.

1. _____ *(far)* scientist is a mineralogist.

2. _____ *(near)* branch of geology is the study of minerals.

3. _____ *(far)* crystals are formed from minerals.

4. _____ *(near)* pencil contains a mineral—graphite.

5. _____ *(near)* rocks contain iron, another important mineral.

47. Those and Them

Those is used to point out something. *Those* may be an adjective or a pronoun. *Them* is always a pronoun. The personal pronoun *them* can never be used as an adjective.

ADJECTIVE NOUN MODIFIED   PRONOUN

Those   jackets are on sale.   **Those** by the escalators are on sale too.

PERSONAL PRONOUN USED AS AN OBJECT

I have two new jackets. I bought them at the sale.

A. Circle the correct word in each sentence.

1. (Those Them) flowers bloom in the fall.

2. Do you know (those them) people?

3. Did you see (those them) boys playing soccer?

4. I have known (those them) for years.

5. Who wrote (those them) adventure stories?

6. Cory saw (those them) on television.

7. I have some of (those them) kinds of stamps in my collection.

8. Jane walked with (those them) through the park.

9. The principal congratulated (those them) for their good grades.

10. (Those Them) sentences were not difficult.

B. Complete each sentence with *those* or *them*.

1. _____ kinds of athletic shoes are expensive.

2. We sent an invitation to _____.

3. Do you prefer these or _____?

4. Are you going to continue fixing _____ two cars?

5. The answers are missing. Can you supply _____?

6. He walked by his friends without noticing _____.

7. Are _____ CDs for sale?

8. My father talked to _____ about moving to Texas.

9. I am not sure if Mom will like these or _____.

10. Deciding between _____ will be difficult.

48. Interrogative Adjectives

> An **interrogative adjective** is used in asking a question. The interrogative adjectives are *which, what,* and *whose. Which* is used in asking about one or more of a specific set of persons or things. *What* is used in asking about people or things that are not necessarily limited to a specific set or group. *Whose* refers to possession.

A. Underline each interrogative adjective. Circle the noun it modifies.

1. Which state in the United States is the largest?

2. In which state was the first U.S. president inaugurated?

3. What animal is on the California state flag?

4. Whose home in Virginia is named Monticello?

5. Which group of islands forms a state?

6. Which state is called the Cradle of Presidents because so many presidents have come from there?

7. Whose residence is located in Washington, D.C.?

8. What city is the capital of Texas?

9. In which city is the Alamo located?

10. In what state was the Declaration of Independence approved?

B. Complete each sentence with an interrogative adjective. For some sentences, more than one answer may be correct.

1. _____ state has Raleigh as its capital?

2. In _____ state is the Sears Tower located?

3. _____ land did Thomas Jefferson purchase for the United States?

4. In _____ year did Texas become a state?

5. In _____ honor was Washington, D.C., named?

6. In _____ state will you find the Empire State Building?

7. _____ portrait is on a dime?

8. In _____ year did World War II end?

9. _____ state is the smallest?

10. _____ state do you live in?

49. Indefinite Adjectives

> **Indefinite adjectives** refer to all or any of a group of persons, places, or things. Some of the most common indefinite adjectives are *all, another, any, both, each, either, every, few, many, most, neither, no, other, several,* and *some*.

Read each proverb. Circle each indefinite adjective and underline the noun that it goes with. One proverb has more than one indefinite adjective.

1. Time cures all things.

2. The rain falls on every roof.

3. A rolling stone gathers no moss.

4. One person's trash is another person's treasure.

5. Many hands make light work.

6. Every bird likes to hear itself sing.

7. Turn the other cheek.

8. Only a fool tests the depth of the water with both feet.

9. No news is good news.

10. Each day provides its own gifts.

11. There are many paths to the top of the mountain, but the view is the same.

12. Some things are better left unsaid.

13. Any plan is bad that cannot be changed.

14. We have other fish to fry.

15. All work and no play make Jack a dull boy.

16. Every dog has its day.

17. Tomorrow is another day.

18. All good things must come to an end.

19. You can't have it both ways.

20. There is no proverb without a grain of truth.

50. Adjective Phrases

> A prepositional phrase is made up of a preposition, its object, and any modifiers of the object. An **adjective phrase** is a prepositional phrase that describes a noun or a pronoun.
>
> **Ancient Rome was a busy city <u>with many large buildings</u>.**

Underline the adjective phrase in each sentence. Circle the noun it goes with.

1. Rich Romans had large, brick houses with red tile roofs.

2. Paintings of flowers often decorated the walls.

3. Mosaics in bright colors covered the floors.

4. Several generations of one family often lived together.

5. A poor family most likely had an apartment of only one room.

6. Such families used water from public fountains.

7. The shops in the neighborhood provided carryout food.

8. The Forum at Rome's center was the main meeting place.

9. It was a place for public speaking.

10 The job of the speakers was to convince the audience.

11. One goal of a Roman boy's education was to become a good speaker.

12. Daily life in the country had a slower pace than city life had.

13. Slaves usually ran the farms of the rich.

14. Families visited their farms to enjoy rest from the city's bustle.

15. Children's toys included board games, kites, and tiny models of people and animals.

16. Boys played various games with balls.

17. Girls had dolls of wax or clay.

18. Romans enjoyed many kinds of entertainment.

19. Most events were free, so people with little money could attend them.

20. The Circus Maximus, a racecourse in Rome, could seat some 250,000 people.

51. Reviewing Adjectives

A. On the line describe the *italicized* adjective as descriptive, numerical, indefinite, demonstrative, or interrogative.

_____ 1. E. L. Konigsburg wrote the book *From the Mixed-up Files of Mrs. Basil E. Frankweiler* about *two* children who run away from home.

_____ 2. In *which* museum does the story take place?

_____ 3. *That* museum is the Metropolitan Museum of Art in New York City.

_____ 4. The children, Claudia and Jamie, have a *wonderful* adventure.

_____ 5. They spend *several* days roaming the hallways of the museum.

_____ 6. The children see a *beautiful* sculpture of an angel.

_____ 7. They want to find out about *that* sculpture.

_____ 8. Is it by the *Italian* artist Michelangelo?

_____ 9. Are they *clever* enough to solve the mystery?

_____ 10. *What* secret lies behind the sculpture?

B. Above each *italicized* adjective write **BN** if the adjective is before a noun or **SC** if it is a subject complement.

11. The room in the museum was *enormous*.

12. An *unusual* object attracted our attention.

13. The object was *Egyptian*.

14. It was like a *small* dollhouse with statues of people inside.

15. The object was for the use of the *dead* person in the afterlife.

C. Underline each indefinite adjective. Circle the noun or nouns it refers to.

16. Many paintings at our art center depict pastoral scenes.

17. There are only a few images of city streets with tall buildings.

18. Among the modern paintings are those of several local artists.

19. Besides the oils and watercolors, our tiny museum tries to display at least one other form of art.

20. I like both forms, oils and watercolors, but I'm also interested in other types of art.

CONTINUED

D. Complete each sentence with *this*, *that*, *these*, or *those*.

21. _____ *(near)* room contains arms and armor.

22. _____ *(far)* chain mail armor differs from _____ *(near)* plate armor.

23. _____ *(near)* helmets all have visors, but _____ *(far)* helmets do not.

24. Look! _____ *(far)* horse is wearing special armor.

25. Even _____ *(near)* shoes are made of metal.

E. Complete each sentence with the correct degree of comparison.

26. What is the _____ (popular) exhibit in the museum?

27. The Egyptian statues are _____ (old) than the Greek statues.

28. Susi thought that the vases were the _____ (pretty) objects in the entire blown-glass display.

29. For Rob the Egyptian room was the _____ (good) part of the museum.

30. For me the armor was _____ (interesting) than the sculpture.

Try It Yourself

Write three sentences about a museum, a park, or another place you visited recently. Describe it. Tell what you found most interesting, most exciting, and so on. Be sure to use adjectives correctly.

_____

_____

_____

Check Your Own Work

Choose a selection from your writing portfolio, your journal, a work in progress, an assignment from another subject, or a letter. Revise it, applying the skills you have reviewed. This checklist will help you.

✔ Have you chosen vivid descriptive adjectives?

✔ Have you been careful to use the correct article?

✔ Have you used correct forms for possessive and demonstrative adjectives?

✔ Have you chosen the correct degree of comparison for adjectives?

52. Principal Parts of Verbs; Verb Phrases

A **verb** shows action or state of being. The principal parts of a verb are the **present**, the **present participle**, the **past**, and the **past participle**. The present participle is formed by adding *-ing* to the base form. The past and the past participle of **regular verbs** are formed by adding *-d* or *-ed* to the base form.

PRESENT	PRESENT PARTICIPLE	PAST	PAST PARTICIPLE
jump	jumping	jumped	jumped
cry	crying	cried	cried
hum	humming	hummed	hummed

A **verb phrase** is two or more verbs used together as a unit. A verb phrase may have one or more **auxiliary**, or **helping**, **verbs** and a main verb. The present participle is often used with auxiliary verbs such as forms of *be*. The past participle is often used with auxiliary verbs such as forms of *has*. Other common auxiliary verbs are *can, could, may, might, should, will,* and the forms of *do*.

We usually <u>wait</u> for my dad here. (present)
We <u>waited</u> here yesterday. (past)
We <u>are waiting</u> for him now. (form of *be* and the present participle)
We <u>have waited</u> for an hour. (form of *have* and the past participle)

Underline the verb or verb phrase in each sentence. Identify the main verb as present, present participle, past, or past participle.

_____ 1. On April 18, 1906, San Francisco experienced a terrible earthquake.

_____ 2. Around 5 a.m. a foreshock occurred.

_____ 3. Within a few seconds the ground was quaking violently.

_____ 4. In less than a minute thousands of buildings had toppled.

_____ 5. Water mains and gas lines shattered.

_____ 6. Soon a huge fire was raging.

_____ 7. By April 21 the fire had destroyed more than 500 city blocks.

_____ 8. About 6,000 people died in the tragedy.

_____ 9. Scientists today warn us about fault lines, probable earthquake sites.

_____ 10. Another such earthquake remains possible.

53. More Verb Phrases

> A verb phrase contains the main verb and an auxiliary, or helping, verb. Following are common auxiliary verbs.
>
> | be | are | has | do | will | can | shall | may |
> |-----|------|------|-----|-------|-------|--------|-------|
> | am | was | have | did | would | could | should | might |
> | is | were | had | | | | | must |
> | | been | | | | | | |

A. Underline each verb phrase.

1. Chimney sweeps have cleaned chimneys for hundreds of years.

2. People should clean their chimneys periodically.

3. Burning wood in a fireplace can leave soot on the chimney walls.

4. After a few years this soot can ignite.

5. A serious fire could be the result.

6. Homeowners must hire a chimney sweep.

7. The number of chimneys has declined.

8. Likewise, the number of chimney cleaners has decreased.

9. Many cities have passed strict laws regarding wood-burning stoves and fireplaces.

10. Traditionally chimney sweeps would be children.

11. They would go into the chimney.

12. Nowadays chimney sweeps are using sophisticated equipment, including video cameras, in their jobs.

13. Chimney cleaners should not be afraid of heights.

14. They often must work on steep roofs.

15. The demand for chimney sweeps usually will be greatest before the start of winter.

B. Circle the auxiliary verb in each sentence.

1. Nursing can be a rewarding profession.

2. Nurses must study for at least two years, and some study for four years.

3. Nurses might work with people of all ages—from babies to the elderly.

4. In the past, nursing had been a profession for women.

5. Now many men as well as women are entering the profession.

Verbs

54. Regular and Irregular Verbs

The past and the past participle of regular verbs are formed by adding *-d* or *-ed* to the present. There is no general rule for forming the past and the past participle of **irregular verbs.** Check a dictionary if you are not sure of these forms.

	PRESENT	PAST	PRESENT PARTICIPLE	PAST PARTICIPLE
REGULAR	**walk**	**walked**	**walking**	**walked**
IRREGULAR	**ride**	**rode**	**riding**	**ridden**

A. Write the present participle, the past, and the past participle of each verb.

PRESENT	PRESENT PARTICIPLE	PAST	PAST PARTICIPLE
1. drift	_____	_____	_____
2. ring	_____	_____	_____
3. rise	_____	_____	_____
4. stop	_____	_____	_____
5. choose	_____	_____	_____
6. talk	_____	_____	_____
7. write	_____	_____	_____
8. make	_____	_____	_____
9. go	_____	_____	_____
10. fly	_____	_____	_____

B. Complete each sentence with the present participle, the past, or the past participle of the verb shown in parentheses.

1. The Old North Church has _____ (stand) in Boston for hundreds of years.

2. One cold night before the American Revolution, Paul Revere was _____ (wait) for a signal.

3. Someone _____ (put) lanterns in the steeple to signal the arrival of British troops.

4. Revere _____ (ride) off to warn the people of the British invasion of Massachusetts.

5. According to tradition, he was _____ (shout) "The British are coming! The British are coming!" as he rode through towns.

55. Lie, Lay and Sit, Set

The verb *lie (lying, lay, lain)* means "to rest or recline." It doesn't have an object.

Please lie on the floor for the warm-up exercise.

The verb *lay (laying, laid, laid)* means "to put in place or position." It takes a direct object.

He laid the books on the table and sat down to study.

The verb *sit (sitting, sat, sat)* means "to have or keep a seat."

Please sit here and have some cookies and milk.

The verb *set (setting, set, set)* means "to put or place in position."

I set the timer for five minutes.

A. Complete each sentence with the correct form of *lie* or *lay*.

1. Matt, please ___lay___ the newspaper on the table.

2. The tourists have ___lain___ on the beach all afternoon.

3. Most of Europe ___lay___ in the north temperate zone.

4. I ___laid___ my glasses somewhere, but I don't remember where.

5. If you are really so sick, I think that you should ___lie___ in bed.

6. Mrs. Greene _____ out the bride's wedding dress and then helped her get ready.

7. Jeff, where did you _____ my coat?

8. My father _____ on the couch to watch TV, but he fell asleep.

9. To relax, you should _____ quietly, close your eyes, and meditate for a few minutes.

10. The cook _____ out a lunch of sandwiches and salads.

B. Complete each sentence with the correct form of *sit* or *set*.

1. Please _____ the buckets in the broom closet.

2. I _____ in the front row so that I can take pictures.

3. We _____ on the 50-yard line at the football game last Sunday!

4. I _____ the two flower pots on either side of the front door.

5. Please _____ that box on the table and help me move this bed.

56. Rise, Raise; Let, Leave; and Teach, Learn

The verb *rise (rising, rose, risen)* means "to ascend or move up."

This road rises very steeply, so cars cannot travel fast.

The verb *raise (raising, raised, raised)* means "to lift up, put up, or elevate."

Please raise your hand if you want to participate.

The verb *let (letting, let, let)* means "to permit or allow."

My dad let me stay up late to watch the movie.

The verb *leave (leaving, left, left)* means "to depart from or to allow to be."

The train left the station on time.

The verb *teach (teaching, taught, taught)* means "to give instruction."

Carla taught her little brother to play catch.

The verb *learn (learning, learned, learned)* means "to receive instruction or to gain knowledge."

He learned to swim when he was 10 years old.

A. Circle the correct verb in parentheses.

1. (Rise Raise) the flag quickly and lower it slowly.

2. (Let Leave) me try that trick.

3. Maureen (left let) for school without her lunch.

4. Please (rise raise) and say the Pledge of Allegiance.

5. My dad (taught learned) me to ride a bicycle.

B. Complete the sentence with the correct verb in the past tense.

1. Slowly the Loch Ness monster _____ from the murky depths.

2. The ship _____ the harbor, on its way to England.

3. My brother _____ me how to play air hockey.

4. The temperature _____ 12 degrees this morning.

5. I _____ school early today to keep a dental appointment.

6. The bridge keeper _____ the bridge so the boat could sail by.

7. We _____ early for the game because traffic was heavy.

8. After I _____ to play chess, I joined the chess club.

9. The speaker _____ from her chair to begin the main address.

10. Dad _____ me set up the tent.

Verbs

57. Transitive Verbs

> A **transitive verb** expresses an action that passes from a doer to a receiver. Every transitive verb has a receiver of its action. The receiver is the direct object.
>
> DOER   TRANSITIVE VERB   RECEIVER (DIRECT OBJECT)
>
> **Eli Whitney**   **invented**   **the cotton gin.**

A. Underline the transitive verb in each sentence. Write **D** above the doer and **R** above the receiver of the action.

1. Eli Whitney earned a college degree in 1792.

2. He learned the newest ideas in science and technology.

3. But he needed a job.

4. Phineas Miller helped him.

5. Miller managed a large plantation in Georgia.

6. Whitney studied the operation of the plantation.

7. English companies wanted American cotton.

8. These companies, however, did not want the seeds in the cotton.

9. Whitney got an idea for a machine.

10. His machine removed all the seeds quickly and easily.

11. Eli Whitney's work helped the English companies.

12. Cotton planters grew more and more cotton.

13. Cotton planters did not pay Whitney for his machines.

14. They simply copied the design of his machine.

15. Later, some states paid him for his invention.

B. Choose the best verb to complete each sentence. Write it in the past tense. Use each verb once. Underline the direct object of each verb.

     fit   invent   make   need   put

1. In 1797 the U.S. government _____ guns for its army.

2. At that time a worker made each part of a gun individually and _____ the parts together.

3. Eli Whitney _____ a system that used machines.

4. Each machine _____ only one part.

5. The parts _____ any gun.

58. Intransitive Verbs

> An **intransitive verb** has no receiver of its action. It does not have a direct object. An intransitive verb may be followed by an adverb or a prepositional phrase.
>
> **Laura Ingalls Wilder <u>wrote</u> about the American Midwest.**

A. Underline the intransitive verb in each sentence.

1. Young Laura Ingalls lived in the Midwest in the late 1800s.

2. Her family farmed.

3. The family's house sat in the woods.

4. Later the family moved from the woods to the prairies farther west.

5. As a young woman, Laura married.

6. Later she wrote about pioneer life.

7. She drew on her experiences as a girl.

8. Her descriptions of the joys and hardships of pioneer life appeal to readers.

9. For example, *Little House on the Prairie* tells about her trip west from Wisconsin in a covered wagon.

10. Laura Ingalls Wilder died in 1957.

B. Underline the intransitive verb(s) in each sentence.

1. The Amazon River starts in the Peruvian Andes.

2. From the Andes it flows east.

3. It travels across northern Brazil.

4. Finally, after almost 4,000 miles, it arrives at the Atlantic Ocean.

5. The river widens and deepens considerably.

6. In fact, large freighters sail in its waters.

7. The Amazon goes through lush rain forests.

8. Thousands of different creatures live in the Amazon.

9. Catfish, electric eels, and piranhas swim in its waters.

10. Millions of unique plants grow in the rain forest along its shore.

Verbs

59. Verbs That Can Be Transitive or Intransitive

Some verbs can be transitive or intransitive, according to their use in a sentence.

TRANSITIVE **Madge ate the cookies.** (*Ate* is transitive because it has a direct object, *cookies*, which is the receiver of the action.)

INTRANSITIVE **We ate at seven o'clock last night.** (*Ate* is intransitive; it does not have a direct object, a receiver of the action.)

A. Underline the verb in each sentence. On the line write **T** if it is transitive or **I** if it is intransitive.

_____ 1. In spring, wildflowers grow along this highway.

_____ 2. We grow flowers in our garden.

_____ 3. The parents hid the presents from their children.

_____ 4. Some animals hide from their predators by means of their color.

_____ 5. Our class sings every morning.

_____ 6. The class sang the national anthem yesterday.

_____ 7. Jana wrote me an e-mail.

_____ 8. Jana always writes on the computer.

_____ 9. Picasso painted priceless masterpieces.

_____ 10. Picasso painted in a variety of styles.

B. Underline the verb in each sentence. On the line write **T** if it is transitive or **I** if it is intransitive. For transitive verbs, circle the receiver (the direct object).

_____ 1. Florence Nightingale, a British woman, founded modern nursing methods in the 1800s.

_____ 2. She rebelled against the idle life of her wealthy family.

_____ 3. Nightingale dedicated her life to the service of others.

_____ 4. With 38 nurses she traveled to Turkey during a war there.

_____ 5. They nursed wounded soldiers.

_____ 6. At first, doctors didn't accept Nightingale's nurses.

_____ 7. Nightingale's work resulted in improvements in hospitals.

_____ 8. The death rate for ill soldiers fell by two thirds.

_____ 9. She raised funds for supplies for soldiers.

_____ 10. She won the respect of the British public for her work.

Verbs

60. Linking Verbs

A linking verb links the subject of a sentence with a subject complement (a noun, a pronoun, or an adjective). The most common linking verbs are forms of *be* (*am, is, are, was,* and *were*).

SUBJECT	LINKING VERB	SUBJECT COMPLEMENT
John F. Kennedy	was	the 35th president of the United States.

The following verbs can also be used as linking verbs: *appear, become, continue, feel, grow, look, remain, seem, smell, sound,* and *taste.*

SUBJECT	LINKING VERB	SUBJECT COMPLEMENT
He	became	president in 1961.

Circle each linking verb. Above each *italicized* subject complement write its part of speech: N for noun, P for pronoun, or A for adjective.

1. John F. Kennedy was *president* from 1961 to 1963.

2. He became an *officer* in the navy during World War II.

3. He was extremely *brave* during the war.

4. After the war he became a *politician*.

5. He became a U.S. *representative* at the age of 29.

6. Kennedy was the country's *president* at 44 years of age.

7. He is *famous* for his inspiring speeches.

8. The founder of the Peace Corps was *he*.

9. Though a war injury caused terrible back pain, he always looked *energetic*.

10. He remained an *advocate* for civil rights for all Americans.

11. He also became an avid *promoter* of space exploration.

12. The leader who set the goal of landing astronauts on the moon was *he*.

13. He was the *author* of two best-selling books.

14. He remained *president* until his assassination in 1963 in Dallas.

15. Americans felt very *sad* about his death.

John F. Kennedy succeeded despite a serious limitation—severe back pain from a war injury. Everyone has limitations of one sort or another. Give an example of a limitation you have and what you can do to overcome it.

61. Reviewing Transitive, Intransitive, and Linking Verbs

A. Underline the verb in each sentence. On the line write **T** if it is transitive, **I** if it is intransitive, or **L** if it is linking.

_____ 1. People throughout much of the world eat salmon.

_____ 2. Fishers catch millions of salmon each year.

_____ 3. Salmon fishing remains an important industry.

_____ 4. Many salmon live in the north part of the Pacific Ocean.

_____ 5. The Atlantic salmon are native to the North Atlantic Ocean.

_____ 6. Chinook are the largest species of salmon.

_____ 7. Salmon lay their eggs in fresh water.

_____ 8. The eggs hatch in fresh water.

_____ 9. Some salmon travel up rivers during mating season.

_____ 10. Salmon fishing is a popular sport on the Pacific coast.

B. Five of these sentences contain linking verbs.
Underline each linking verb and circle its complement.

11. The salmon is famous for its long and difficult journeys.

12. At spawning time salmon swim upstream.

13. They can leap over 10-foot waterfalls.

14. The male salmon is the protector of the female during spawning.

15. She deposits her eggs in a stream bed.

16. The male then fertilizes the eggs.

17. The eggs hatch after three or four months.

18. The young salmon are food for many predators.

19. The young salmon travel to the ocean and grow large.

20. Species of salmon sometimes become rare because of overfishing.

Verbs

Name _____

62. Simple Tenses

The **simple present tense** tells about an action that happens again and again and about things that are general truths.
> **Russia now <u>elects</u> its leader.**

The **simple past tense** tells about an action that happened in the past.
> **Czars <u>ruled</u> imperial Russia.**

The **simple future tense** tells about an action that will happen in the future.
> **Continuing reforms <u>will help</u> Russia to a better government.**

A. Underline the verb in each sentence. Write the tense on the line.

_____ 1. Czars had power in Russia until 1917.

_____ 2. In 1917, revolutionaries overthrew the czar.

_____ 3. Communists became dominant in the new government.

_____ 4. Communists controlled Russia for more than 70 years.

_____ 5. In 1991 the Soviet Union ended.

_____ 6. Russia became a republic.

_____ 7. The Communist party no longer rules in Russia.

_____ 8. The Russian people want a democratic government.

_____ 9. Will the Russians build a democratic system?

_____ 10. The answer will appear in the years to come.

B. Complete each sentence with the tense of the verb indicated.

control 1. OPEC, the Organization of Petroleum Exporting Countries, _____ the oil production of many nations. (*present*)

join 2. Many oil-producing countries _____ OPEC. (*past*)

meet 3. Representatives from each of the member countries _____ from time to time to discuss oil production. (*present*)

discuss 4. They _____ the levels of oil production. (*present*)

decide 5. Sometimes they _____ to lower production. (*present*)

make 6. Such a decision _____ oil prices increase. (*future*)

cut 7. In the 1970s OPEC _____ production. (*past*)

go 8. As a result, gas prices in the United States _____ up. (*past*)

be 9. There _____ long lines of cars at the gas pumps. (*past*)

reduce 10. _____ new car designs _____ the need for gasoline? (*future*)

63. Progressive Tenses

The **progressive tenses** are formed with the present participle and a form of *be*. The **present progressive tense** tells about something that is happening right now. It uses the present tense of *be (am, is, are)* and the present participle.

The children <u>are reciting</u> nursery rhymes.

The **past progressive tense** tells about something that was happening in the past. It uses the past tense of *be (was, were)* and the present participle.

They <u>were sitting</u> in a circle at the start of the program.

The **future progressive tense** tells about something that will be happening in the future. It uses *will be, is going to be,* or *are going to be* with the present participle.

The teacher <u>will be asking</u> several students to perform.
Are the children <u>going to be illustrating</u> their favorite rhymes?

Verbs

A. Underline each verb in the progressive tense. On the line tell if the verb is in the present progressive tense, the past progressive tense, or the future progressive tense.

_____ 1. Mrs. Johnson is reading nursery rhymes to the children in preschool.

_____ 2. She will be displaying posters that go with what she reads.

_____ 3. The children are enjoying the rhymes.

_____ 4. When I was growing up, I liked to listen to nursery rhymes too.

_____ 5. While the teacher was reading, I recited the words with her.

B. Complete each sentence with the correct progressive tense of the verb at the left.

go   1. Jack and Jill _____ up the hill
          with an empty pail. *(past)*

grow   2. Mary, Mary, Quite Contrary _____
          silver bells in her garden. *(present)*

sit   3. While Humpty Dumpty _____
          on a wall, he had a great fall. *(past)*

try   4. All the king's horses and all the king's men _____
          to put him together again. *(present)*

eat   5. Little Miss Muffett _____ curds and whey while she sat on
          a tuffet. *(past)*

fall   6. According to the old rhyme, London Bridge _____ down. *(present)*

laugh 7. The little boy _____ as the cow jumps over the moon. *(future)*

sit   8. Little Jack Horner _____ in a corner as he ate a pie. *(past)*

get   9. Mother Hubbard _____ her dog a bone. *(future)*

fly   10. Look! Four and twenty blackbirds _____ out of the pie! *(present)*

64. Perfect Tenses

The **perfect tenses** are formed with the past participle and a form of *have.* The **present perfect tense** tells about an action that happened at some indefinite time in the past or an action that started in the past and continues into the present time. It uses the present tense of *have (has, have)* and the past participle.

Marge <u>has made</u> a delicious chocolate cake.

The **past perfect tense** tells about a past action that was completed before another past action started. It uses the past tense of *have (had)* and the past participle.

Homer <u>had eaten</u> three slices before we even got one.

A. Underline each verb in the perfect tense. On the line tell whether the verb is in the present perfect tense or the past perfect tense.

_____ 1. My mother's family has had a family reunion for many years.

_____ 2. My mother's great-grandfather had started the tradition long before I was born.

_____ 3. My family has gone to the reunion for many years.

_____ 4. We have had a lot of fun every time we attended!

_____ 5. The reunions have been at the local picnic grounds for the last five years.

_____ 6. Cousin Ona has won the sack race many times, but I am determined to win the next race.

_____ 7. Earlier this year no one had remembered that the picnic grounds needed to be reserved.

_____ 8. By the time we arrived, other people had taken our usual spot.

_____ 9. After everyone from our family had arrived, we decided to hold the picnic in our backyard.

_____ 10. Aunt Joan had prepared seven quarts of potato salad because she expected a huge crowd.

B. Complete each sentence with the correct perfect tense of the verb at the left.

ask   1. Many eager fans _____ the famous movie star for her autograph. *(present)*

try   2. She _____ to avoid them. *(present)*

avoid   3. She _____ leaving her hotel room. *(present)*

gather   4. Anxiously, the fans _____ outside her hotel as afternoon approached. *(past)*

hope   5. They _____ to get her autograph before she left for the Academy Awards ceremony. *(past)*

Verbs

65. More Perfect Tenses

Complete each sentence with the indicated tense.

sing   1. Our school's chorus _____ on TV. (present perfect)

sing   2. It _____ the same song in a concert held
        last month. (past perfect)

choose 3. We _____ the date for the picnic. (present perfect)

choose 4. We _____ the same picnic grove we used
        two years ago. (past perfect)

damage 5. Floods _____ the town before this year's record flood
        nearly submerged it. (past perfect)

damage 6. This year's flood _____ the entire downtown area.
        (present perfect)

finish 7. I _____ not _____ all my homework yet. (present perfect)

finish 8. I _____ my science project before I started my
        math assignment. (past perfect)

ride   9. I _____ never _____ the new roller coaster at
        Adventure Park. (present perfect)

ride   10. Once, after I _____ a roller coaster three times
        in a row, I got sick. (past perfect)

eat   11. Allison _____ not _____ sushi before she tasted
        it last week. (past perfect)

eat   12. She _____ sushi twice since then! She really likes it!
        (present perfect)

take   13. My brother _____ a few piano lessons,
        and he can play several songs. (present perfect)

take   14. He _____ never _____ a music
        lesson before he attended the concert. (past perfect)

travel 15. My friends _____ in
        a helicopter several times. (present perfect)

travel 16. They _____ not _____ in
        one until they received free tickets. (past perfect)

see   17. I _____ never _____ a live shark
        before I went to the aquarium yesterday. (past perfect)

see   18. Now I _____ both very large and
        very small sharks. (present perfect)

break   19. The students _____ three beakers in the lab.
        (present perfect)

break   20. Before they dropped the beakers today, they _____ never
        _____ a single one. (past perfect)

Verbs

66. Reviewing Tenses

Complete each sentence with the tense of the verb indicated in parentheses.

interest   1. The planet Mars _____ humans for thousands of years. *(present perfect)*

be   2. Mars _____ Earth's neighbor and the seventh-largest planet in the solar system. *(simple present)*

find   3. In the 1800s people thought that scientists _____ canals on Mars and that this discovery provided proof of life there. *(past perfect)*

see   4. What the scientists _____ were channels, not dug-out canals. *(past perfect)*

write   5. Long before humans launched spacecraft, science fiction writers _____ about life on Mars. *(past progressive)*

write   6. H. G. Wells _____ *The War of the Worlds,* a book about an invasion of Earth by creatures from Mars. *(simple past)*

invade   7. In Ray Bradbury's stories *The Martian Chronicles,* inhabitants from Earth _____ Mars. *(past progressive)*

send   8. Since the 1960s several countries _____ spacecraft to explore Mars. *(present perfect)*

pass   9. In 1965 the U.S. spacecraft *Mariner 4* _____ within 9,920 kilometers of the planet's surface. *(simple past)*

take   10. It _____ 22 close-up photos that showed a cratered surface. *(simple past)*

conduct   11. Landers from the United States, *Viking 1* and *Viking 2,* _____ experiments on Mars soil during the 1970s. *(simple past)*

conduct   12. Currently the United States _____ _____ a series of probes of Mars with the *Odyssey* spacecraft. *(present progressive)*

continue   13. The spacecraft, which reached Mars in 2001, _____ to provide valuable information about the planet. *(future)*

wonder   14. People still _____ about the possibility of life on Mars. *(present progressive)*

find   15. _____ these spacecraft _____ any life there? *(future)*

67. Subject-Verb Agreement

A verb agrees with its subject in person and number. The base form of a verb is used for the present tense with both singular and plural subjects. The present tense verb for a third person singular subject, however, is formed by adding -s or -es to the base form of the verb.

THIRD PERSON SINGULAR **A senator serves for six years.**

THIRD PERSON PLURAL **Two senators from each state serve in Congress.**

Verbs

A. Underline the verb in each sentence. In the first column write **S** if the subject is singular or **P** if it is plural. In the second column identify the person of the subject: **1** for first person, **2** for second person, and **3** for third person.

	NUMBER	PERSON
1. We study U.S. government in school.	_____	_____
2. The president serves for four years.	_____	_____
3. Citizens elect representatives for two-year terms.	_____	_____
4. The representatives have the possibility of reelection.	_____	_____
5. Supreme Court justices get lifetime appointments.	_____	_____
6. The Senate confirms the justices.	_____	_____
7. Some politicians stay in office for many years.	_____	_____
8. Strom Thurmond of South Carolina was a member of Congress for nearly 50 years.	_____	_____
9. Are you surprised by that fact?	_____	_____
10. He was in the U.S. Senate from 1954 to 2003.	_____	_____

B. If the underlined noun is singular, make it plural. If it is plural, make it singular. Change the verb to agree with the new subject. Write your answers on the lines.

	NEW SUBJECT	NEW VERB
1. A president takes on many responsibilities.	_____	_____
2. The presidents hold the executive power.	_____	_____
3. A senator meets with voters.	_____	_____
4. Members of the House meet with voters.	_____	_____
5. A citizen needs to express opinions.	_____	_____

68. More Subject-Verb Agreement

A subject and its verb must always agree in person and number. When a sentence starts with *there* and a form of the verb *be (is, are, was, were),* the subject follows the verb. The form of *be* must agree with the subject.

There was an English colony in Massachusetts in the 1600s.
There were several children on board the *Mayflower.*

A. Underline the subject in each sentence. Circle the correct verb in parentheses.

1. Among the early settlers (was were) Pilgrims from England.

2. Plymouth (was were) the site of the first permanent settlement of Europeans in New England.

3. Nowadays this old town (is are) a tourist attraction.

4. Many visitors (come comes) to see the town.

5. These tourists (see sees) Plymouth Plantation, a reconstruction of the original settlement.

6. The old houses (is are) also popular attractions.

7. This historic place (has have) more than a tourist-based economy, however.

8. Boatyards (line lines) the shore.

9. Fishing (was were) important during much of Plymouth's past.

10. Many fishing boats (continue continues) to dock in Plymouth Harbor.

B. Circle the correct verb in parentheses.

1. There (was were) more than 100 Pilgrims on the *Mayflower.*

2. The Pilgrims arrived in Plymouth in December. There (was were) many problems for them at first.

3. There (was were) no place to live. They had to clear the land and build a fort.

4. There (was were) very little food that winter.

5. There (is are) a replica of the *Mayflower* in Plymouth Harbor today.

6. There (is are) many things to see and do in Plymouth.

7. There (is are) many restored colonial houses.

8. There (is are) also a large state forest nearby.

9. There (is are) a monument to the Pilgrims in the center of Plymouth.

10. There (is are) several museums, including a wax museum.

Verbs

69. Doesn't and Don't; You as the Subject

If the subject is in the third person singular, use *doesn't*. For all other third person singular and plural subjects, use *don't*.

THIRD PERSON SINGULAR	Alice doesn't get up early.
OTHER SINGULAR AND PLURAL	I don't have an alarm clock
	You don't have to wake me, however.
	The children don't get up early.

Use *are* and *were* with the subject *you*, whether *you* is singular or plural.

SINGULAR	You are always late, Jennifer.
PLURAL	You are late again, Jennifer and Carla.

A. Complete each sentence with *doesn't* or *don't*.

1. A pine tree _____ shed its needles in winter.

2. A pine tree's needles _____ get brown either.

3. An evergreen tree _____ lose its color in winter.

4. During winter most other trees in northern climates _____ keep their leaves.

5. When a tree loses its leaves in fall, it _____ die.

6. The tree _____ produce new leaves until spring.

7. All trees will die, however, if they _____ get water.

8. If rain _____ provide enough moisture, even a pine tree may turn brown.

9. During a drought, trees will die if people _____ water them.

10. We _____ need to water the tree in our yard this summer because we have had plenty of rain.

B. Circle the correct verb in parentheses.

1. (Is Are) you going on a field trip today with your class?

2. You (is are) the best speller in class.

3. Sally and Nancy, (is are) you going to wear your jackets?

4. Jim, (was were) you in the library this afternoon?

5. (Were Was) you at the game yesterday?

70. Agreement with Compound Subjects Connected by *And*

> Compound subjects connected by the word *and* usually require a verb that agrees with a plural subject.
>
> **England and France** <u>were</u> allies in World War I.

A. Circle the correct verb in parentheses.

1. Germany and Austria-Hungary (was were) allies in World War I.

2. Germany and France (was were) enemies in World Wars I and II.

3. World War I and World War II (was were) so terrible that the countries of Europe realized they needed to work together.

4. Belgium, France, West Germany, Italy, Luxembourg, and the Netherlands (was were) the first members of the original European organization in 1958.

5. England and Spain (was were) admitted later.

6. England, France, Germany, and Italy now (work works) together in the European Union.

7. Austria, Germany, England, and France (is are) no longer enemies.

8. Political cooperation and economic unity (represent represents) basic goals of the European Union.

9. People and goods (move moves) freely among the countries in the Union.

10. As a result, war and conflict (has have) become less likely in Europe.

B. Circle the correct verb. Add words to complete the sentences.

1. World War I and World War II (was were) _____.

2. England, France, and Germany (has have) _____.

3. The European Union and the United States (is are) _____.

4. Belgium and Luxembourg (has have) _____.

5. France and Germany (share shares) _____.

Verbs

71. Agreement with Indefinite Pronouns

The indefinite pronouns *each, either, neither, anyone, no one, anybody, nobody, everyone, everybody, someone,* and *somebody* are always singular. They require verbs that agree with singular subjects.

> **Each** of the students **has** a responsibility in the classroom.
> **Someone** **unlocks** the school doors at 8.
> Nearly **everyone** **arrives** by 8:45.

Verbs

A. Complete each sentence with the correct present tense form of the verb at the left.

know   1. Everyone _____ our school's routine.

say   2. Everybody _____ the Pledge of Allegiance in the morning.

raise   3. Someone _____ the flag before classes start.

sing   4. Everyone _____ the national anthem before a major sports event.

take   5. Each of the teachers _____ attendance.

lower   6. At the end of the day someone _____ the flag.

follow   7. Each of the classes _____ an end-of-the-day routine too.

erase   8. Somebody _____ the boards daily.

go   9. Almost everyone _____ home at 3:30.

leave   10. The principal and the assistant principal stay later; neither of them _____ until five o'clock.

B. Write about the routine at your school. Circle the correct verb. Add words to complete the sentences.

1. Almost everybody (arrives arrive) _____.

2. Hardly anybody (come comes) _____.

3. Somebody (clean cleans) _____.

4. Everyone (is are) _____.

5. Everybody (sing sings) _____.

72. Agreement with Special Nouns

Nouns such as *deer, fish, sheep, trout, salmon, cod, moose, corps,* and certain proper nouns such as *Portuguese, Chinese, Swiss,* and *Iroquois* have the same form in the singular and the plural. The sense of the sentence indicates whether the subject is singular or plural.

A. Underline the subject in each sentence. Write **S** above the subject if it is singular and **P** if it is plural. Circle the correct verb in parentheses.

1. A famous Sioux (was were) Crazy Horse, who led his tribe in a war against the U.S. government.

2. Red salmon (is are) caught in Puget Sound.

3. The Iroquois (was were) allies of the British in the wars of the 1700s.

4. Look! A deer (is are) eating grass in the backyard.

5. The Spanish (lives live) on the Iberian Peninsula.

6. The Sioux (belong belongs) to the group called the Plains Indians.

7. Trout (live lives) mainly in fresh water.

8. A moose (is are) a member of the deer family.

9. Reindeer (was were) brought from Siberia to Alaska.

10. Some sheep (is are) waiting to be sheared.

11. Deer (is are) timid by nature.

12. These fish (is are) such a lovely orange-red color.

13. A Portuguese, Bartolomeu Dias, (is are) remembered for his explorations.

14. The Chinese (inhabit inhabits) the world's most populous country.

15. A small goldfish (was were) raised by the class in this fish tank.

B. Circle the correct verb. Add words to complete the sentence.

1. This deer (live lives) _____.

2. A Sioux (is are) _____.

3. The Chinese (live lives) _____.

4. That small sheep (has have) _____.

5. Trout (swim swims) _____.

73. Reviewing Subject-Verb Agreement

A. Circle the correct verb in parentheses.

1. African Americans (celebrate celebrates) a holiday in December.

2. (Are Is) you familiar with the holiday?

3. Its name (is are) Kwanzaa.

4. There (is are) seven days of celebration.

5. Each of the days (is are) devoted to a different principle, such as unity, creativity, or faith.

6. On December 31 everybody (participates participate) in a feast.

7. There (is are) special plays and speeches at the feast.

8. Children (doesn't don't) receive gifts until January 1.

9. The Swahili (celebrate celebrates) a similar harvest holiday, as do other African peoples.

10. The feast (doesn't don't) have a long history in this country; it began in 1966.

B. Complete each sentence with the correct present tense form of the verb at the left.

house   11. This building _____ stray dogs and cats.

want   12. Each of the children _____ to use the computer.

be   13. There _____ 10 tomatoes on the counter.

be   14. _____ you ready for the class play?

be   15. The flowers and the vase _____ on the coffee table.

be   16. Everyone _____ going to get an ice-cream sundae.

have   17. The French _____ many great paintings in their museums.

be   18. Look! There _____ a shooting star!

need   19. This fish _____ some food in its tank.

crow   20. A rooster _____ every morning.

74. Active and Passive Voice

Voice shows whether the subject of a sentence is the doer or the **receiver** of the action expressed by the verb. When a verb is in the **active voice,** the subject is the doer of the action. When a verb is in the **passive voice,** the subject is the receiver of the action.

ACTIVE VOICE   **Ancient Rome <u>had</u> many public baths.**
PASSIVE VOICE   **The baths <u>were visited</u> by both men and women.**

A. Each sentence is written in the passive voice. Rewrite it in the active voice.

1. Admission was charged by the owner of the bath.

   _____

2. Steam rooms and saunas were provided by some baths.

   _____

3. Hair-cutting salons were featured at other baths.

   _____

4. A variety of goods was sold by shopkeepers.

   _____

5. The baths were used by most Romans every day.

   _____

B. Each sentence is written in the active voice. Rewrite it in the passive voice.

1. Shops lined the streets of Rome.

   _____

2. Men wore cotton or wool tunics.

   _____

3. Slaves taught children reading, writing, and arithmetic.

   _____

4. They used pebbles to do math problems.

   _____

5. Their mothers taught girls to spin and weave.

   _____

Verbs

75. Indicative Mood

Mood shows the manner in which an action or a state of being is expressed. The **indicative mood** of a verb is used when the speaker is making a statement or asking a question. Most sentences are in the indicative mood. Verbs in the indicative mood can be in any tense, and they can be active or passive.

> **What are the big cats of Africa?** (question, simple present tense)
> **She read about lions, leopards, and cheetahs.** (statement, simple past tense, active)
> **These cats have been hunted for their skins.** (statement, present perfect tense, passive)

Underline the verb in the indicative mood in each sentence. Write the tense on the line. Add the correct end punctuation.

_____ 1. Do you know about the small cats of Africa

_____ 2. I have learned about several kinds

_____ 3. The African wild cat has the largest territorial range

_____ 4. African wild cats were the ancestors of domestic cats

_____ 5. We are checking the map for locations of the African golden cat

_____ 6. I had never heard of servals before

_____ 7. Where do they live

_____ 8. They have been seen throughout Sub-Saharan Africa

_____ 9. One observer watched a serval near a pond

_____ 10. By the end of three hours, the cat had eaten 28 frogs

_____ 11. Caracals are the largest of the small cats

_____ 12. How much do they weigh

_____ 13. They have been known to weigh 40 pounds

_____ 14. Caracals are famous for catching low-flying birds

_____ 15. Had you heard of any other small African cats

_____ 16. Earlier I was reading about sand cats

_____ 17. These cats are found in the deserts of North Africa

_____ 18. How have they adapted to the severe desert climate

_____ 19. Thick hair protects the bottom of their feet

_____ 20. Sand cats go without water for long periods of time

76. Emphatic Form of the Indicative Mood

The **emphatic form** of the indicative mood gives special force to a simple present or past tense verb. To make an emphatic form in the present tense, use *do* or *does* before the base form of the verb in a statement. To make an emphatic form in the past tense, use *did* before the base form of the verb.

Many people do want to know more about Antarctica.
The United States did establish a research station there in the 1950s.

A. Underline the verb phrase in the emphatic form in each sentence. On the line write whether the verb phrase is in the present tense or the past tense.

_____ 1. Antarctica does have the coldest weather on earth.

_____ 2. Once the temperature did drop to –126.9° Fahrenheit.

_____ 3. Summer temperatures do average around freezing.

_____ 4. The cold does make it almost impossible for humans to live there.

_____ 5. Several species of penguins and seals do spend part of the year in Antarctica.

_____ 6. The ancient Greeks did think there was land to the far south.

_____ 7. In 1773 Captain James Cook did sail around the continent, but he could not land because of the ice.

_____ 8. Historians do believe that Captain John Davis landed on Antarctica in 1821.

_____ 9. In 1911 explorers did reach the South Pole.

_____ 10. Scientists today do study Antarctica's climate and geology.

B. Rewrite each sentence. Change the *italicized* verb to the emphatic form.

1. Two kinds of fish *thrive* in the cold waters around Antarctica.

_____

2. Fishing fleets *wanted* to know more about these fish.

_____

3. Scientists *equipped* seals with video cameras.

_____

4. These "seal cams" *helped* the scientists learn about the fish.

_____

5. Some animals *have* unusual jobs!

_____

Verbs

Name _____

77. Imperative Mood

The **imperative mood** is used to express a command or a request. To form the imperative mood, use the base form of a verb. The subject of an imperative sentence is understood to be the second person pronoun, *you*.

> **Tell me how to find the North Star.** **Locate the Big Dipper.**
> **Please focus the telescope.** **Find a protractor.**

A command can be given in the first person by using *let's (let us)* before the base form of a verb.

> **Let's buy a star chart.**

Rewrite each sentence in the imperative mood.

1. You can find out your latitude.

    _____

2. First you should tie a 15-inch piece of string to the middle of the flat side of a protractor.

    _____

3. Then you need to tie an eraser or other small weight to the loose end of the string.

    _____

4. You should then hold the straight edge of the protractor near your eye.

    _____

5. You must be sure that the curved side is down.

    _____

6. You have to point the protractor directly at the North Star.

    _____

7. Next you need to pinch the string against the side of the protractor to mark the angle.

    _____

    _____

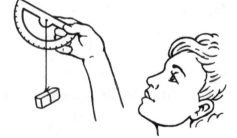

8. You should then read the angle on the protractor.

    _____

9. You have to use the number that is less than 90°.

    _____

10. Finally you need to subtract that number from 90° to find your latitude.

    _____

Verbs

78. Subjunctive Mood

The **subjunctive mood** is used in several ways: (1) to express a wish or desire; (2) to express a request, a command, or a suggestion after the word *that;* or (3) to express something that is contrary to fact (not true). The subjunctive refers to something that is hoped or wished rather than what actually is.

For the verb *be,* the common forms of the subjunctive are *be* and *were. Be* is used with verbs of command, request, or suggestion. Otherwise, *were* is used. In many sentences with *if* clauses, the auxiliary verb *would* is used in the second clause.

I wish I <u>were</u> able to play the piano better. (a wish)
My mom suggested that I <u>be</u> more willing to practice.
(a suggestion after *that*)
If I <u>were</u> a concert pianist, I would make her proud.
(something contrary to fact)

A. Underline the subjunctive verb or verb phrase in each sentence. Write **W** for a wish or desire; **R** for a request, command, or suggestion after *that;* or **C** for something contrary to fact.

_____ 1. I wish my dog were better behaved.

_____ 2. If she were better behaved, I would enter her in the dog show.

_____ 3. My mother suggested I be more diligent about training her.

_____ 4. If she were still a puppy, I would take her to obedience school.

_____ 5. If I were more patient, I'd work with her every day.

_____ 6. My dad insists that she be kept off the furniture.

_____ 7. He wishes she were kept in the kitchen at all times.

_____ 8. If she were smaller, the problem would not be as bad.

_____ 9. I begged that he be more tolerant with her.

_____ 10. I wish we were all in agreement on this matter.

B. Underline the correct form of the verb for the subjunctive and then complete each sentence with your own idea.

1. If I (was were) President of the United States, I would

   _____.

2. I wish my school (was were) _____.

3. I recommend that top athletes (be are) _____.

4. I wish my class (was were) _____.

5. If I (was were) a better singer, I'd _____.

79. Modal Auxiliaries

Modal auxiliaries are used to express possibility, permission, ability, necessity, obligation, intention, and willingness. They are followed by main verbs in the base form. Common modal auxiliaries are *may, might, can, could, must, should, will,* and *would.*

POSSIBILITY	We <u>might watch</u> a movie tonight.
PERMISSION	Mom says we <u>may make</u> some popcorn.
ABILITY	We <u>can pop</u> it right in the bag in the microwave.
NECESSITY	We <u>must leave</u> the kitchen as neat as we found it.
OBLIGATION	We <u>should clean</u> the inside of the microwave.
INTENTION	I <u>will wash</u> the bowls and glasses.
WILLINGNESS	<u>Would</u> you please help me with the beverages?

A. Underline the modal auxiliary in each sentence once. Underline the main verb twice. On the line write what the verb phrase expresses—possibility, permission, ability, necessity, obligation, intention, or willingness.

_____ 1. We must prepare for our yard sale tomorrow.

_____ 2. We should sort all the things into categories.

_____ 3. I will separate the books into fiction and nonfiction.

_____ 4. Would you arrange the CDs and DVDs?

_____ 5. Dad said we may sell this old lawn mower.

B. Complete each sentence with a modal auxiliary, according to the meaning given in parentheses. More than one modal auxiliary may be correct for some sentences.

1. _____ you like a job as a babysitter? *(willingness)*

2. Every babysitter _____ take a first-aid class. *(obligation)*

3. A babysitter _____ watch the children at all times. *(necessity)*

4. Some parents _____ allow you to take the children outdoors. *(possibility)*

5. Others _____ tell you to stay in the house. *(possibility)*

6. A babysitter _____ follow the parent's instructions. *(necessity)*

7. What _____ you do to entertain the children? *(intention)*

8. You _____ plan some activities for them. *(possibility)*

9. You _____ amuse children with some simple items. *(ability)*

10. You _____ want to take a game you can play with them. *(possibility)*

Verbs

Name _____

80. Reviewing Verbs

A. Underline the verb or verb phrase in each sentence. If there is an auxiliary verb, write it on the line.

_____ 1. Michelangelo lived in Italy.

_____ 2. You can see one of his famous works, the *Pietà*, in Rome.

_____ 3. You will feel amazement at the sculpture's power.

_____ 4. The sculpture has traveled to the United States.

_____ 5. People could see it in New York at a World's Fair in the 1960s.

B. Write the forms for each verb.

	PRESENT PARTICIPLE	PAST	PAST PARTICIPLE
6. sing	_____	_____	_____
7. walk	_____	_____	_____
8. grow	_____	_____	_____
9. drop	_____	_____	_____
10. put	_____	_____	_____

C. Underline the verb in each sentence. On the line write **T** if the verb is transitive or **I** if it is intransitive.

_____ 11. Michelangelo carved magnificent statues.

_____ 12. He also painted.

_____ 13. He painted the ceiling of the Sistine Chapel in Rome.

_____ 14. Michelangelo depicted the story of creation and other Bible stories on the ceiling of the chapel.

_____ 15. He died in 1564.

D. Read each sentence. On the line write **IN** for indicative, **IM** for imperative, or **SU** for subjunctive.

_____ 16. Have you seen any of Michelangelo's works?

_____ 17. His statue of David is in Florence, Italy.

_____ 18. Look at a picture of it on the Internet.

_____ 19. I wish I were in Italy.

_____ 20. If I were in Italy, I would go to Florence.

CONTINUED

Name _____

E. On the line identify the tense of the *italicized* verb in each sentence—
simple present, simple past, future, present progressive, past progressive,
present perfect, or past perfect.

_____ 21. People *have known* about peanuts since
ancient times.

_____ 22. A peanut *is* not actually a nut.

_____ 23. Peanuts *belong* to the legume—bean—family.

_____ 24. Peanuts *were growing* in the Americas
long before the Europeans settled here.

_____ 25. They *had grown* in South America before
they were introduced to North America.

_____ 26. In the United States, peanuts first *grew*
in the South.

_____ 27. George Washington Carver *created*
more than 300 products from peanuts—
including printer's ink and soap.

_____ 28. People *have eaten* peanuts as snacks
since the 1860s.

_____ 29. Peanut butter *has teamed* with jelly in
sandwiches since the 1920s.

_____ 30. People *will enjoy* peanut products for years to come.

Try It Yourself

Write three sentences about a painting or a sculpture you like. Describe
the work of art. Tell why you like it. Be sure to use verbs correctly.

_____

_____

_____

Check Your Own Work

Choose a selection from your writing portfolio, your journal, a work in progress, an
assignment from another subject, or a letter. Revise it, applying the skills you have
reviewed. This checklist will help you.

✔ Have you used correct forms of the irregular and regular verbs?

✔ Have you been careful when you used any of the troublesome verbs?

✔ Have you correctly formed verbs in the different tenses?

✔ Do all of your subjects and verbs agree in number?

Verbs

81. Adverbs of Time

> An **adverb** is a word that describes, or modifies, a verb, an adjective, or another adverb. **Adverbs of time** answer the question when or how often. They usually modify verbs.
>
> **She has <u>already</u> read a few books of myths.** (modifies *has read*)
> **She <u>often</u> reads Aesop's fables.** (modifies *reads*)
>
> Adverbs of time include *again, already, always, before, early, ever, finally, first, frequently, immediately, later, never, now, often, once, recently, seldom, sometimes, soon, still, today,* and *usually.*

A. Circle the adverb of time in each sentence. Underline the verb it modifies.

1. People have always been curious about the natural world.

2. Ancient myths—or stories—often attempted to explain things in nature.

3. Ancient people, including the Greeks, frequently created stories about the origins of the world and the things in it.

4. Later the ancient Romans borrowed myths from the Greeks.

5. The main characters of these myths were usually gods or heroes.

6. Have you ever seen a horse with wings?

7. Well, the mythical horse Pegasus sometimes flew through the air.

8. The names of the planets still reflect the influence of mythology.

9. First, the telling of myths was part of an oral tradition.

10. Finally, poets such as Homer recorded the myths.

B. Circle the correct adverb of time.

1. We have (already ever) begun our study of classical art.

2. Many classical sculptures are (now early) in the British Museum.

3. The sculpture of ancient Greece has (seldom yesterday) been equaled.

4. Visitors to Greece can see examples of classical statues (today ever).

5. (Once Always) I saw a picture of the Venus de Milo, an ancient statue of a goddess. Its arms are missing.

6. People (often before) wonder what it would have looked like with arms.

7. Another famous statue, the Winged Victory, (now never) lacks its head.

8. People (usually already) think that classical statues were white.

9. Scholars believe that the ancients (always now) painted the statues.

10. When the statues were found, the paint had (already never) worn off.

82. Adverbs of Place

> **Adverbs of place** answer the question where. They usually modify verbs.
>
> **Please don't play catch <u>inside</u>.** (modifies *play*)
> **You can walk <u>there</u>.** (modifies *can walk*)
>
> Adverbs of place include *above, away, back, below, down, far, forward, here, in, inside, outside, there, up,* and *within.*

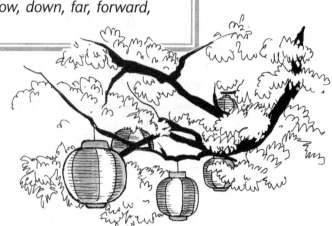

A. Circle each adverb of place.
Underline the verb it modifies.

1. The eagle soared upward in its flight.

2. The little boy's dog ran away.

3. Bright stars twinkled overhead.

4. List all your suggestions below.

5. Orioles build nests high in the trees.

6. Beautiful paper lanterns hung here and there among the trees.

7. Because of the blizzard we didn't go outside for two days.

8. Place the table here, please.

9. The boy went inside for his boots.

10. Please look up when you finish the exercise.

B. Circle the correct adverb of place in each sentence.

1. Our neighbors have just moved (away downward).

2. Please look (inside outside) and see if it is raining.

3. You've gone the wrong way. You need to walk
   (back here) two blocks.

4. We looked (away around) for the missing books.

5. The batter swung too (low down) and missed the ball. He was out!

6. The two new polar bears are (upward there) on the rocks.

7. The kittens should not be left (outside below) in the rain.

8. Please sign your name (here forward), Ms. Bergen.

9. Don't look (down far) or you'll get dizzy.

10. We were so cold that we had to go (inside far).

83. Adverbs of Manner

Adverbs of manner answer the question how or in what manner. They usually modify verbs. Many, but not all, adverbs of manner end in *-ly*. Three common exceptions are *fast*, *well*, and *hard*.

> **She learned math quickly.** (modifies *learned*)
> **She worked hard all afternoon.** (modifies *worked*)

Some adverbs of manner are *anxiously, bravely, cheerfully, correctly, courageously, diligently, fast, gracefully, kindly, steadily, swiftly, truthfully,* and *unexpectedly.*

A. Write an adverb of manner for each adjective.

1. proud _____
2. excited _____
3. happy _____
4. soft _____
5. intelligent _____

6. easy _____
7. beautiful _____
8. diligent _____
9. tireless _____
10. thoughtful _____

B. Circle each adverb of manner. Underline the verb it modifies.

1. Barbara McClintock, a scientist, worked carefully and determinedly.

2. She deservedly won a Nobel Prize for Medicine in 1983 for her work.

3. An intelligent woman, she quickly earned a Ph.D.—in two years.

4. Genetics interested her, and she studied cells intently.

5. She worked hard in her laboratory.

6. She painstakingly examined the genetic structure of corn.

7. In 1931 she brilliantly explained a genetic process called crossing-over, which was the discovery that earned her the Nobel Prize.

8. Many scientists foolishly rejected her ideas.

9. She patiently rechecked her research.

10. Later discoveries by other scientists clearly supported her work.

Barbara McClintock continued to work even when others said that she was wrong. She showed that she had tremendous confidence in herself. Name one or two ways you can show that you have confidence in yourself.

84. Adverbs of Degree

Adverbs of degree answer the question how much or how little.
They may modify verbs, adjectives, or other adverbs.

> He was **barely** moving. (modifies *was moving*, a verb)
> The story is **rather** interesting. (modifies *interesting*, an adjective)
> He traveled **quite** extensively. (modifies *extensively*, an adverb)

Adverbs of degree include *almost, awfully, barely, extraordinarily, extremely, fairly, fully, greatly, hardly, incredibly, merely, much, partly, quite, rather, really, scarcely, somewhat, terribly, too,* and *very.*

Circle each adverb of degree. Underline the word it modifies.
Identify the word that is modified by writing **V** above it if it is a verb,
Adj if it is an adjective, or **Adv** if it is an adverb.

1. Spain is rather famous for the exploration of North and South America.

2. Spaniards did not discover America; they merely explored it.

3. The civilizations in the Americas were quite complex.

4. Some Spanish explorers and writers have left fairly concise accounts of the civilizations in the Americas.

5. Spain's exploration in other parts of the world is hardly discussed.

6. Ruy Gonzalez de Clavijo, however, rather daringly traveled to the Middle East in the 15th century.

7. Gonzalez, a Spanish diplomat, went from Spain to Turkey and Iran in 1403, a time when travel was awfully difficult.

8. He met Tamburlaine, an Islamic king, who was very powerful.

9. Tamburlaine had built an extremely large empire in Asia.

10. He was a fierce fighter who was greatly feared by his enemies.

11. Tamburlaine treated his enemies terribly cruelly.

12. He wanted to make his capital at Samarkand incredibly beautiful.

13. The mosque there has extraordinarily lovely mosaics of turquoise and gold.

14. Gonzalez wrote a really wonderful account of his visit to Tamburlaine's kingdom.

15. Many people have never heard about this quite unusual trip.

85. Adverbs of Affirmation and Negation

Adverbs of affirmation and negation tell whether a statement is true or false. The **adverbs of affirmation** include *allegedly, indeed, positively, undoubtedly,* and *yes*.

You undoubtedly know who Annie Oakley is.

The **adverbs of negation** include *no, not,* and *never*.

I have never heard of her.

A. Underline each adverb of affirmation or negation.
Above each write **A** if it indicates affirmation or **N** if it indicates negation.

1. Yes, Annie Oakley was an American sharpshooter and entertainer.

2. Indeed, she could shoot dimes tossed into the air.

3. She was a star of Buffalo Bill Cody's Wild West show, and her sharpshooting feats never failed to amaze audiences.

4. Her real name was not Annie Oakley; it was Phoebe Ann Moses.

5. Undoubtedly, she was an amazing person.

B. Underline each adverb. Write on the line what it indicates—**T** for time, **P** for place, **M** for manner, **D** for degree, **A** for affirmation, or **N** for negation.

_____ 1. The Northwest Ordinance of 1787 had a very important role in the history of Ohio, Indiana, Illinois, Michigan, and Wisconsin.

_____ 2. First, the Ordinance organized the distribution of land in the territory.

_____ 3. The land there was divided according to a grid system.

_____ 4. Land was carefully divided into townships— squares of six miles on each side.

_____ 5. Next, each township was divided into individual sections—one mile on each side.

_____ 6. One of these sections was always set aside for schools.

_____ 7. People quickly bought the individual sections.

_____ 8. The Ordinance also carefully specified the procedure for new states to join the Union.

_____ 9. Finally, the Ordinance granted key civil rights to the residents of the territory, including freedom of religion.

_____ 10. Indeed, the Northwest Ordinance of 1787 prohibited slavery in the area.

Adverbs

89

86. Comparative and Superlative Adverbs

Some adverbs can be compared. The **comparative degree** compares the quality of two actions or conditions. The **superlative degree** compares three or more. To form the comparative degree or the superlative degree of adverbs that do not end in *-ly*, add *-er* or *-est*. To form the comparative or superlative of adverbs that end in *-ly*, add *more* or *most* (or *less* or *least*) before the adverb.

> **If I use a computer, I can work faster than I can if I use a typewriter.**
> **A computer can do this work more efficiently than a typewriter can.**

Two common adverbs that have irregular comparative and superlative forms are *well* and *badly: well, better, best; badly, worse, worst.*

A. On the lines write the comparative and the superlative forms of each adverb.

	COMPARATIVE	SUPERLATIVE
1. early	_____	_____
2. wisely	_____	_____
3. badly	_____	_____
4. fast	_____	_____
5. gracefully	_____	_____

B. On the line write the comparative form of the adverb at the left.

early   1. The day of the field trip we got up _____ than usual.

fast   2. Mercury spins on its axis _____ than Venus does.

late   3. Our guests arrived _____ than we expected.

clearly   4. He speaks _____ than he writes.

slowly   5. Please speak _____.

C. On the line write the superlative form of the adverb at the left.

far   1. Andrew threw the Frisbee _____.

clearly   2. Of all the students in our class, Brice talks _____.

fast   3. Marlene finished the assignment _____.

near   4. Melody is sitting _____ to the blackboard.

carefully   5. Of all the bus drivers, Mr. Pulaski drives _____.

Adverbs

87. More Comparative and Superlative Adverbs

A. Circle the correct form of the adverb.

1. The bus left (later   latest) than we expected.

2. Doug cooks (more often   most often) than he used to.

3. Can you walk (faster   fastest) than that?

4. The bells rang (louder   loudest) than usual.

5. The last surfer rode the waves (more gracefully   most gracefully).

6. Please examine this fossil (more carefully   most carefully) of all.

7. Jason cooks (worse   worst) than Allen does.

8. Jonathan skated (more skillfully   most skillfully) than Bert did.

9. Marty works (more diligently   most diligently) of all the students.

10. You are making a lot of noise, Karen and Linda. Please work (more quietly   most quietly).

B. Complete each sentence with the correct form of the adverb.

closely   1. We looked _____ at the gems than at the other rock specimens in the exhibit.

easily   2. Of all the math problems in the assignment, I solved this one _____.

well   3. The basketball team played _____ today than it did yesterday.

fast   4. Please work _____.

clearly   5. Kate was selected for the play because she speaks _____ than Cindy does.

violently   6. The volcano erupted _____ than it had in decades.

hard   7. Because he had worked _____ all year, Tyrone was happy when summer vacation arrived.

politely   8. Of all the clerks, Ms. Grimes deals with customers _____.

softly   9. Please play that music _____.

rapid   10. Express mail is delivered _____ than regular mail.

Adverbs

88. Adverbs and Adjectives

An adjective describes a noun or a pronoun. It may precede or follow the word it describes, or it may follow a linking verb. An adverb modifies a verb, an adjective, or another adverb. An adverb may appear at various locations in a sentence.

  NOUN   ADJECTIVE
That sound from the radio isn't really clear.

  VERB   ADVERB
Actors must say their lines clearly.

Do not confuse the adjective *good* and the adverb *well.* The comparative form of both words is *better,* and the superlative of both is *best (good, better best; well, better, best).*

Circle the correct word in parentheses.
Write on the line whether the word is
used as an adjective or an adverb.

_____ 1. During the Revolution, Tories were (loyal loyally) to Britain.

_____ 2. The crossing guard always looks (cheerful cheerfully) in the morning.

_____ 3. Rita plays the violin (good well).

_____ 4. The new bus driver seems quite (capable capably).

_____ 5. Please move that computer (careful carefully) so you don't drop it.

_____ 6. The child (forgetful forgetfully) left her toy on the lawn.

_____ 7. The teacher explained the math problems very (good well).

_____ 8. The oatmeal tasted (delicious deliciously).

_____ 9. This pink and orange sunset is really (beautiful beautifully).

_____ 10. Marcy is always (thoughtful thoughtfully) of others.

_____ 11. The students worked (quiet quietly) on their own.

_____ 12. Mrs. Lee (generous generously) donated a million dollars to charity.

_____ 13. The nurses in that hospital are very (helpful helpfully).

_____ 14. The director spoke (angry angrily) to the cast during rehearsals.

_____ 15. Margie (polite politely) thanked her grandmother for the gift.

Adverbs

Name _____

89. Negative Words

Using two negative words where only one is needed is called a double negative. If a sentence already has a negative word, avoid using another negative word. The most common negative adverbs are *no, not,* and *never.* The adverbs *barely, hardly,* and *scarcely* have a negative sense and should not be used with other negative terms.

INCORRECT	Never eat no wild mushrooms.
CORRECT	Never eat any wild mushrooms.
INCORRECT	I can't hardly reach the top shelf.
CORRECT	I can hardly reach the top shelf.
	I can't reach the top shelf.

A. Underline the correct word in parentheses.

1. There are things people should (never ever) do around the house.
2. Don't insert (any no) more than two plugs into one outlet.
3. Don't (ever never) stick a knife into a toaster that is plugged in.
4. Never run (any no) wires under a rug or carpet.
5. (Never Ever) touch an electrical wire with wet hands.
6. Don't (ever never) put your finger directly into an electrical outlet.
7. (No one Anyone) should use a power tool unless he or she is wearing safety glasses.
8. Don't leave (any no) toys or shoes on the stairs.
9. (Ever Never) keep household cleansers within reach of small children.
10. (Any No) sharp objects should be left where toddlers can find them.

B. Rewrite the following sentences to correct any errors in the use of negatives.

1. We couldn't barely move the heavy couch.

   _____

2. She didn't have no way to get to the library.

   _____

3. There's not scarcely enough time to finish.

   _____

4. I can't hardly read that sign.

   _____

5. I haven't never any energy left.

   _____

90. Adverb Phrases and Clauses

A **prepositional phrase** is made up of a preposition, its object, and any modifiers of the object. A prepositional phrase used as an adverb is an **adverb phrase.** Adverb phrases tell when, where, how, how much, why, or to what extent.

The children are playing <u>in the park.</u>

A **clause** is a group of words that has a subject and a predicate. A dependent clause cannot stand on its own as a sentence. A dependent clause used as an adverb is an **adverb clause.** An adverb clause answers the same questions as an adverb phrase.

They will come home <u>after they finish their game.</u>

A. Underline the adverb phrase in each sentence. Circle the word(s) it modifies.

1. Many American families move during the summer.

2. The children will start classes in the fall.

3. Some children worry about their new schools.

4. Many children write their worries in their journals.

5. As soon as possible, the children become familiar with their new surroundings.

6. They may ride their bikes around their neighborhoods.

7. They research their new cities on the Internet.

8. They search online for local radio stations.

9. They learn about parks and community activities.

10. They leave their e-mail addresses with their old friends.

B. Underline the adverb clause in each sentence. Circle the word(s) it modifies.

1. Before we moved, I downloaded a map of our new neighborhood.

2. I drew the route to school so that I wouldn't get lost.

3. Since I belong to a scout troop, I contacted a troop in my new town.

4. I took photos of my old room because I want to remember it.

5. I bought an autograph book so that all my friends could sign it.

6. Whenever I feel sad, I read what they wrote.

7. While I was packing, I selected toys to donate to charity.

8. After the truck was loaded, I walked around the neighborhood one last time.

9. I will call my friends if I feel lonely.

10. Although they live in a different town, I know how to contact them.

Name _____

91. Reviewing Adverbs

A. Underline each adverb. Write on the line what it indicates—**T** for time, **P** for place, **M** for manner, **D** for degree, **A** for affirmation, or **N** for negation.

_____ 1. We saw a great baseball game recently.

_____ 2. Runners from the opposing team were on first and second bases, and we waited anxiously for the pitcher to throw the ball.

_____ 3. Our pitcher threw the ball hard.

_____ 4. The batter swung low and missed.

_____ 5. The runner unexpectedly tried to steal third base.

_____ 6. The runner did not make it. The catcher threw the ball to the player at third base, who tagged the runner.

_____ 7. The fans jumped to their feet excitedly.

_____ 8. I jumped up with the others!

_____ 9. The crowd really cheered!

_____ 10. Yes, our team held its lead!

B. Circle the correct adverb in parentheses. On the line write **C** if the adverb is comparative or **S** if it is superlative.

_____ 11. Sound travels quickly. It travels (faster fastest) of all in solid materials.

_____ 12. Sound travels (more slowly most slowly) through gases than through solid materials.

_____ 13. Light travels (more quickly most quickly) than sound does.

_____ 14. Light travels (better best) through a transparent solid like clear glass than through a translucent solid such as frosted glass.

_____ 15. Compared with heat and sound, light travels through space (faster fastest).

C. Circle the correct word in parentheses. Write on the line whether it is an adjective or an adverb.

_____ 16. Marta looked at the large package (hopeful hopefully).

_____ 17. She was (eager eagerly) to see the contents.

_____ 18. Her mother (careful carefully) opened the mysterious box.

_____ 19. Marta waited (patient patiently) while her mother pulled out a present.

_____ 20. Marta felt (happy happily) about the beautiful book her grandmother had sent her.

CONTINUED

D. Underline each adverb phrase. Circle the word(s) it modifies.

21. We visited many places on our trip.

22. We drove through Redwood National Park.

23. Many huge trees grow in this park.

24. Some trees have lived for centuries.

25. You can actually drive through one large tree.

E. Underline each adverb clause. Circle the word(s) it modifies.

26. Many people went to California after gold was discovered there.

27. Although some people found gold, others made money in different ways.

28. When Levi Strauss got there, he made pants for miners.

29. The miners liked the pants because they were strong and cheap.

30. Whenever you wear Levi's, you should think of Levi Strauss.

F. Circle the correct word in parentheses.

31. My friends have (ever never) been to California.

32. Has no one (ever never) visited a movie studio?

33. We didn't see (any no) movie stars when we were there.

34. There wasn't (any no) sight more impressive than the redwoods.

35. We had (ever never) seen such tall trees before.

Try It Yourself

Write three sentences about an exciting event that you attended or that you saw on TV. Be sure to use adverbs correctly.

_____

_____

_____

Check Your Own Work

Choose a selection from your writing portfolio, your journal, a work in progress, an assignment from another subject, or a letter. Revise it, applying the skills you have reviewed. This checklist will help you.

✔ Have you included appropriate adverbs of time, place, and manner?

✔ Have you used the correct form for adverbs used in comparisons?

✔ Have you used adverb forms, and not adjective forms, where they are needed?

✔ Have you followed the rules for avoiding double negatives?

92. Simple Subjects and Simple Predicates

A sentence has a subject and a predicate. The **simple subject** is the noun or pronoun that names the person, place, or thing the sentence is about. The **simple predicate** is the verb that tells what the subject does or is.

SIMPLE SUBJECT	SIMPLE PREDICATE
Water	evaporates.
Cold water	evaporates slowly.
Water at the boiling point	evaporates quickly.

A. Write the simple subject and the simple predicate of each sentence in the appropriate column.

SIMPLE SUBJECT   SIMPLE PREDICATE

1. Plants need water. _____ _____

2. Plants in the desert get water in many ways. _____ _____

3. A cactus stores water in its thick stem. _____ _____

4. Some plants have long roots. _____ _____

5. These long roots reach water deep underground. _____ _____

6. Flowers bloom after a rainstorm. _____ _____

7. Animals need water too. _____ _____

8. Many animals in the desert rest all day. _____ _____

9. Foxes hunt in the cool evenings. _____ _____

10. The food of some animals provides them with water. _____ _____

B. Draw one line under the simple subject. Draw two lines under the simple predicate.

1. Animals in the ocean obtain oxygen and food from the water around them.

2. Some of these animals hunt for food.

3. Other kinds always stay in one place.

4. Microscopic animals in the water are an important source of food.

5. Whales filter these animals from seawater for food.

93. Complete Subjects and Complete Predicates

The **complete subject** of a sentence is the simple subject with all the words that describe it. The **complete predicate** contains the verb, its modifiers, and its complements or objects.

COMPLETE SUBJECT	COMPLETE PREDICATE
The islands of the West Indies	**lie between North and South America.**

SIMPLE SUBJECT	SIMPLE PREDICATE
islands	**lie**

Draw a vertical line between the complete subject and the complete predicate. Draw one line under the simple subject. Draw two lines under the simple predicate.

1. The West Indies separate the Caribbean Sea from the Atlantic Ocean.

2. The chain of islands is about 3,200 kilometers long.

3. The West Indies' climate is tropical.

4. Destruction of the native forests occurred during plantation days.

5. Sugar-plantation owners needed wood for hot fires for sugar refining.

6. Some countries passed laws to protect the forests.

7. The people of these islands come from many parts of the world.

8. Languages spoken on the islands include English, French, Spanish, and Dutch.

9. Many people on the islands are descendants of slaves.

10. Caribbean countries depend on farming for part of their income.

11. Farmers on these tropical islands raise several different kinds of crops.

12. Exports from the islands include sugar, bananas, and coffee.

13. The islands import large amounts of wheat.

14. Tourism brings a lot of business to the islands.

15. The island of Jamaica is a popular tourist destination.

Sentences

94. Compound Subjects and Compound Predicates

> A **compound subject** consists of more than one simple subject.
>   **Beatrix Potter** and **Beverly Cleary** are famous authors of children's books.
>
> A **compound predicate** consists of more than one simple predicate.
>   Their books **amuse** and **delight** children everywhere.

A. Each sentence has a compound subject or a compound predicate.
Draw a vertical line between the subject and the predicate.
Underline the compound subject or predicate.

1. The owl and the pussycat went to sea
   in a beautiful pea-green boat.

2. The owl looked up to the stars above
   and sang to a small guitar.

3. The walrus and the carpenter were walking
   close at hand.

4. Jack and Jill went up the hill for a pail of water.

5. Little Jack Horner stuck in his thumb and pulled out a plum.

B. Underline each compound subject. Circle each compound predicate.

1. Beatrix Potter wrote and illustrated her own stories.

2. Peter Rabbit and his family are the characters in one story.

3. Flopsy, Mopsy, and Cottontail lived with Peter under the root of a big fir tree.

4. Mr. McGregor and Mrs. McGregor planted and weeded their garden.

5. Mrs. Rabbit shopped for food and cooked the meals.

6. The four little bunnies hopped down the lane and gathered blackberries.

7. Mr. McGregor shouted and waved his rake.

8. Peter ran away and squeezed under the gate.

9. Flopsy, Mopsy, and Cottontail ate blackberries and drank milk.

10. Peter and his mother had tea for supper.

95. Natural and Inverted Order

A sentence is in **natural order** when the verb follows the subject.

SUBJECT   VERB

The Spanish conquerors came onto the island.

A sentence is in **inverted order** when the verb or an auxiliary verb comes before the subject.

VERB   SUBJECT

Onto the island came the Spanish conquerors.

VERB   SUBJECT   VERB

When did the Spanish conquerors come onto the island?

A. Underline the subject once and the verb twice. On the line write **N** if the sentence is in natural order or **I** if it is in inverted order.

_____ 1. Europeans first came to the Americas in the 11th century.

_____ 2. To the Americas came explorers, missionaries, and settlers.

_____ 3. Spain conquered much of Mexico, Central America, and South America.

_____ 4. In the rest of North America lived settlers from England and France.

_____ 5. The newly arrived Europeans uprooted and destroyed the Native American civilizations.

_____ 6. Westward pushed the North American pioneers.

_____ 7. To reservations went Native Americans.

_____ 8. The Cherokee traveled from Georgia to the West on a journey later called the Trail of Tears.

_____ 9. Were the Sioux moved to reservations?

_____ 10. Early settlers focused on their needs for more territory and not on the needs of the native people.

B. Five of the sentences in Part A are in inverted order. Rewrite them in natural order on the lines.

1. _____

2. _____

3. _____

4. _____

5. _____

Sentences

96. More Natural and Inverted Order

A. Rewrite each sentence, using inverted order.
Use inverted order in questions where indicated.

1. The game of baseball developed from an English game called rounders. *(question)*

_____

2. The annual All-Star Game began in 1933.

_____

3. Wrigley Field, the home of the Chicago Cubs, is here.

_____

4. The Baseball Hall of Fame stands in Cooperstown, New York.

_____

5. Hank Aaron's bat is among the baseball relics in the hall. *(question)*

_____

_____

B. Rewrite each sentence, using natural order.

1. Does he know when the sport of baseball began?

_____

_____

2. Named to the Baseball Hall of Fame in 1973
was Roberto Clemente.

_____

3. Into the air leapt the star outfielder.

_____

4. In the bottom of the ninth inning came the last desperate attempt to win.

_____

5. Into home plate slid the runner with the winning run.

_____

97. Declarative Sentences and Interrogative Sentences

A **declarative sentence** makes a statement.
A declarative sentence ends with a period.

A volcano is an opening in the earth's crust.

An **interrogative sentence** asks a question.
An interrogative sentence ends with a question mark.

Why do volcanoes erupt?

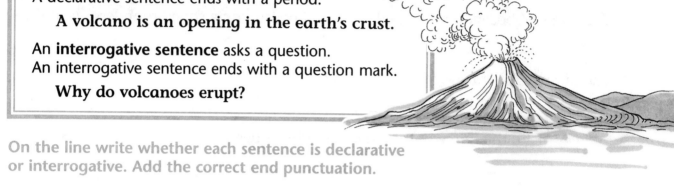

On the line write whether each sentence is declarative or interrogative. Add the correct end punctuation.

_____ 1. Volcanoes have magma chambers inside them

_____ 2. What is magma

_____ 3. Magma is molten rock

_____ 4. Volcanoes erupt because of density and pressure

_____ 5. How does density affect a volcano

_____ 6. Magma is less dense than the surrounding rocks are

_____ 7. Bubbles of gas form in the magma

_____ 8. What happens when the bubbles rise

_____ 9. The bubbles exert tremendous pressure on the rock

_____ 10. The pressure pushes the magma and rock out of the earth

_____ 11. Is there molten rock on the surface of the earth

_____ 12. Lava is molten rock that reaches the earth's surface

_____ 13. In some volcanoes lava oozes out slowly

_____ 14. Do some volcanoes explode violently

_____ 15. Rock, ash, and cinders can shoot out of openings

_____ 16. How often do volcanoes erupt

_____ 17. Some volcanoes erupt more often than others

_____ 18. On average, Kilauea in Hawaii erupts every 3.95 years

_____ 19. Mount St. Helens in Washington state erupted in 1980

_____ 20. It hadn't erupted in more than 120 years

Sentences

98. Imperative Sentences and Exclamatory Sentences

An **imperative sentence** gives a command or makes a request.
An imperative sentence ends with a period.

Explain the nature of friction.

An **exclamatory sentence** expresses a strong emotion.
An exclamatory sentence ends with an exclamation mark.

That's truly amazing!

A. Underline the sentences that are imperative.

1. Friction makes moving in water difficult.

2. Take a smooth rubber ball and a tennis ball.

3. Put a little water into a shallow bowl.

4. Try spinning each ball in the bowl.

5. Which one spins more easily?

6. Write your results in your journal.

7. The rubber ball is smoother than the tennis ball.

8. The smooth surface causes less friction.

9. That's why a fast boat generally has a smooth body.

10. Think of another experiment dealing with friction.

B. On the line write whether each sentence is imperative or exclamatory.
Add the correct end punctuation.

_____ 1. Get a glass jar with a lid

_____ 2. Have some soap and water ready

_____ 3. Screw the cover on the jar as tightly as you can

_____ 4. Be careful

_____ 5. Wow, that's really tight

_____ 6. Wet your hands with the soap and water

_____ 7. Try to take the lid off the jar

_____ 8. It's impossible

_____ 9. State an observation about friction

_____ 10. Think really hard

Name _____

99. The Four Kinds of Sentences

A sentence can be declarative, interrogative, imperative, or exclamatory.

On the line identify each sentence as declarative, interrogative, imperative, or exclamatory. Add the correct end punctuation.

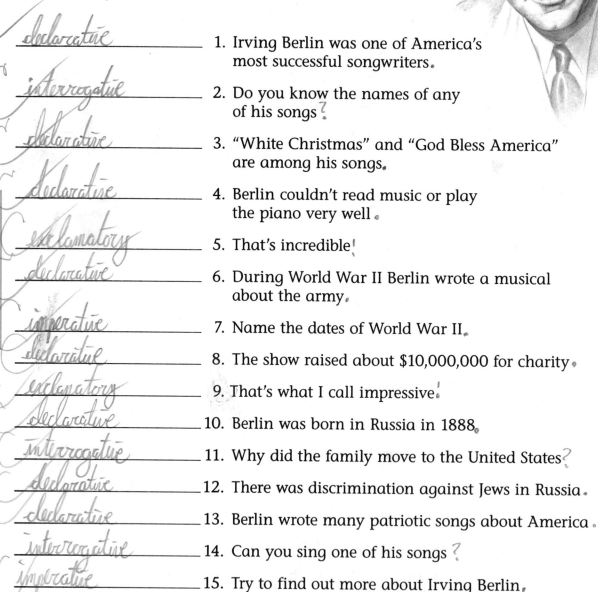

declarative — 1. Irving Berlin was one of America's most successful songwriters.

interrogative — 2. Do you know the names of any of his songs?

declarative — 3. "White Christmas" and "God Bless America" are among his songs.

declarative — 4. Berlin couldn't read music or play the piano very well.

exclamatory — 5. That's incredible!

declarative — 6. During World War II Berlin wrote a musical about the army.

imperative — 7. Name the dates of World War II.

declarative — 8. The show raised about $10,000,000 for charity.

exclamatory — 9. That's what I call impressive!

declarative — 10. Berlin was born in Russia in 1888.

interrogative — 11. Why did the family move to the United States?

declarative — 12. There was discrimination against Jews in Russia.

declarative — 13. Berlin wrote many patriotic songs about America.

interrogative — 14. Can you sing one of his songs?

imperative — 15. Try to find out more about Irving Berlin.

Irving Berlin believed that music could cheer people up and give them courage. Give an example of how you can cheer people up and give them courage.

Sentences

Name _____

100. Simple Sentences

A **simple sentence** contains a subject and a predicate.
Either or both may be compound.

SUBJECT	PREDICATE
Lyndon Johnson	had a long record of public service.
Johnson and his wife, Lady Bird,	were from Texas.
Johnson	worked hard for civil rights laws and tried to help poor Americans.

Underline each simple subject once. Underline each simple predicate twice. Identify each compound subject and compound predicate by writing **C** in the appropriate column.

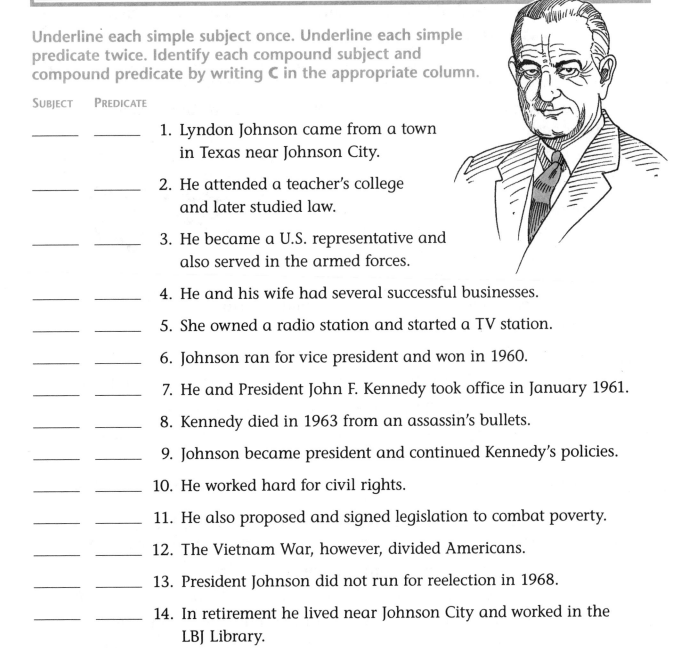

SUBJECT   PREDICATE

_____ _____ 1. Lyndon Johnson came from a town in Texas near Johnson City.

_____ _____ 2. He attended a teacher's college and later studied law.

_____ _____ 3. He became a U.S. representative and also served in the armed forces.

_____ _____ 4. He and his wife had several successful businesses.

_____ _____ 5. She owned a radio station and started a TV station.

_____ _____ 6. Johnson ran for vice president and won in 1960.

_____ _____ 7. He and President John F. Kennedy took office in January 1961.

_____ _____ 8. Kennedy died in 1963 from an assassin's bullets.

_____ _____ 9. Johnson became president and continued Kennedy's policies.

_____ _____ 10. He worked hard for civil rights.

_____ _____ 11. He also proposed and signed legislation to combat poverty.

_____ _____ 12. The Vietnam War, however, divided Americans.

_____ _____ 13. President Johnson did not run for reelection in 1968.

_____ _____ 14. In retirement he lived near Johnson City and worked in the LBJ Library.

_____ _____ 15. Johnson died in 1973 and was buried on his ranch in Texas.

101. Compound Sentences

> A **compound sentence** contains two or more independent clauses.
> An independent clause has a subject and a verb and can stand on
> its own as a sentence. Independent clauses are usually connected by
> the coordinating conjunctions *and, but, or, nor, yet,* and *so.*
>
> INDEPENDENT CLAUSE   INDEPENDENT CLAUSE
> **Albany is the capital of New York, but New York City is its largest city.**
>
> Instead of a coordinating conjunction a semicolon may be used between
> independent clauses.
>
> **Albany is the capital of New York; New York City is its largest city.**

A. Underline the simple subjects once and the verbs twice. Circle the coordinating conjunction or the semicolon that connects the independent clauses.

1. New York City has the largest population of any city in the United States, but Los Angeles covers more land.

2. New York City is the largest city in the United States, and Los Angeles is the second largest.

3. New York City sits on a number of islands; the most famous island is Manhattan.

4. San Francisco is located in northern California, and Los Angeles is located in southern California.

5. Los Angeles has many TV and film studios, and San Francisco has a large computer industry.

6. San Francisco is fairly hilly; Los Angeles is more level.

7. Los Angeles and New York City are located on coasts; Chicago is inland.

8. New York City has many tall buildings, but Chicago has taller ones.

9. In Los Angeles many people drive to work, and in New York many people use subways.

10. Our family toured New York city last year, but I am anxious to visit it again.

B. On the line write **S** if the sentence is a simple sentence or **C** if the sentence is a compound sentence. Add the correct punctuation to each compound sentence.

_____ 1. New York is famous for its large number of theaters.

_____ 2. New York has several orchestras and it has several ballet companies too.

_____ 3. The Statue of Liberty is in New York Harbor millions of people visit it yearly.

_____ 4. New York City is a business center and is the home of many banks.

_____ 5. The New York skyline is famous and Central Park is a great escape from the hustle and bustle of the city.

Sentences

102. More Compound Sentences

Combine each pair of simple sentences to form a compound sentence.
Use a comma before the coordinating conjunctions *and*, *but*, *or*, *nor*, *yet*, and *so*.

1. The United States celebrates its Independence Day on July 4. Peru celebrates its Independence Day on July 28.

   _____

   _____

2. Americans might attend fireworks displays on July 4. They might stay home and watch them on TV.

   _____

   _____

3. Many countries celebrate New Year's Day on January 1. In Muslim countries the new year begins on the first day of the month of Muharram.

   _____

   _____

4. On New Year's Day many Americans attend football games or watch them on TV. On that day many Chinese visit friends and exchange gifts.

   _____

   _____

5. In the United States Mother's Day is in May. Father's Day is in June.

   _____

6. Carnival in Brazil is right before Lent. Mardi Gras in New Orleans is at the same time.

   _____

7. In most western countries Sunday is a holiday. In Islamic countries Friday is a holiday.

   _____

   _____

8. Queen Elizabeth's real birthday is April 21. People celebrate her birthday on the third Saturday in June, when the weather in England is pleasant.

   _____

   _____

9. The birthday of the Queen of England is a holiday in England. This day is not a holiday in the United States.

   _____

   _____

10. The Christian holiday of Easter is usually in April. Sometimes it is in March.

    _____

Sentences

103. Reviewing Simple and Compound Sentences

On the line write **S** if a sentence is simple or **C** if it is compound.

_____ 1. Fairy tales are fictitious, but they are excellent stories.

_____ 2. In Germany the Grimm Brothers collected many fairy tales.

_____ 3. Jacob Grimm was born in 1785, and Wilhelm Grimm was born in 1786.

_____ 4. Jacob and Wilhelm at first studied law in college.

_____ 5. They developed a love of German folk traditions from their teachers, and they began to study folktales and fairy stories.

_____ 6. Many of these stories were quite old; some dated from the Middle Ages and earlier.

_____ 7. The brothers became lawyers, but they remained interested in these stories.

_____ 8. By 1814 they had given up their legal careers and were pursuing their studies of folktales.

_____ 9. They did not make much money, and they had to spend their earnings carefully.

_____ 10. They collected large numbers of stories and published them in a book.

_____ 11. Some of the stories in their collection are versions of the Cinderella tale and the Rapunzel tale.

_____ 12. This book was popular, and thousands of people bought copies.

_____ 13. In 1840 the king of Prussia invited the brothers to Berlin.

_____ 14. In Berlin the king paid them a generous salary, and they could focus on their work.

_____ 15. Wilhelm and Jacob also began to study linguistics and published an important book about the German language.

_____ 16. They also started work on a German dictionary, but the task was too large for them.

_____ 17. Wilhelm finished only to the letter D by the time of his death, and Jacob reached only F.

_____ 18. Their collections of stories and their other books made the brothers famous.

_____ 19. They received prizes and honors.

_____ 20. They are most beloved for their collections of fairy stories and folktales.

Sentences

Name _____

104. Prepositions

> A **preposition** is a word that shows the relation of a noun or a pronoun to another word in a sentence. The noun or pronoun that follows the preposition is the **object of the preposition**.
>
>   PREPOSITION   OBJECT
>
>   **Frederick Douglass made many contributions   to   the country.**
>
> Common prepositions are *at, after, against, by, for, from, in, into, of, on, to, with,* and *without.*

Circle each preposition.

1. Frederick Douglass was one of the most important human rights leaders of the 19th century.

2. He was born into slavery in Maryland with the name Frederick Bailey.

3. Shortly after his birth, his owners separated him from his mother, who was a slave.

4. His mother was moved some 20 miles away, a long distance in those days.

5. When he was seven or eight years old, his owner had him work for the Auld family in Baltimore.

6. At that time he learned reading from Mrs. Auld.

7. When children in the neighborhood finished their books, they gave them to young Frederick.

8. Against all odds Frederick continued teaching himself.

9. When he was older, Frederick escaped on a train, and he lived in New York as a free person.

10. He changed his name to Douglass.

11. Douglass began speaking against slavery.

12. He became a consultant to President Abraham Lincoln.

13. He helped convince Lincoln that slaves should be freed if they fought in the Civil War against the South.

14. After the war Douglass pressed for full civil rights for freed slaves.

15. Frederick Douglass became the first African American diplomat when he was appointed U.S. ambassador to Haiti.

Frederick Douglass worked hard to educate himself and then used his education to help others. Give an example of how you can use your education to help others.

105. Prepositional Phrases

> A **prepositional phrase** consists of a preposition, a noun or a pronoun that is its object, and any modifiers of the object.
>
> **The Missouri River is the longest river <u>in the United States</u>.**

A. Underline each prepositional phrase. Circle each preposition.

1. The Mississippi River starts in Minnesota near the Canadian border.
2. It flows toward the south.
3. South of St. Paul, Minnesota, the river becomes wide enough and deep enough for vessels.
4. Two major tributaries, the Missouri River and the Ohio River, flow into it.
5. The Missouri River joins the Mississippi River at St. Louis.
6. After the river is joined by the Ohio River, it becomes huge.
7. In many places, the river is a mile and a half from shore to shore.
8. This river is one of the busiest commercial waterways in the world.
9. The river floods in spring, which often causes damage to cities near the river.
10. The Mississippi empties into the Gulf of Mexico through a huge delta.

B. Use each preposition in a prepositional phrase about a body of water near your home. Circle the object of the preposition.

1. through _____
2. near _____
3. from _____
4. over _____
5. into _____

C. Write a sentence, using each phrase from Part B.

1. _____
2. _____
3. _____
4. _____
5. _____

Name _____

106. At and To, Between and Among

> *At* shows presence in. *To* shows motion toward.
>
> **Ed and Bert are <u>at</u> the museum. They're going <u>to</u> the gold exhibit.**
>
> Use *between* to speak of two persons, places, or things.
> Use *among* to speak of more than two.
>
> **There is much trade <u>between</u> the United States and Canada.**
> **There is trade <u>among</u> the United States, Canada, and Mexico.**

A. Complete each sentence with *at* or *to.*

1. Our class took a trip _____ New York.

2. We spent the morning _____ the
   United Nations (UN) headquarters.

3. We sailed _____ the Statue of Liberty.

4. We stood _____ the foot of the statue.

5. Then we walked _____ the top.

6. After that we went _____ Ellis Island.

7. Many immigrants _____ the United States arrived at Ellis Island.

8. We also went _____ the Metropolitan Museum of Art.

9. We saw many important exhibits _____ the museum.

10. We also saw animals _____ the zoo in Central Park.

B. Complete each sentence with *between* or *among.*

1. The United Nations works for peace _____ all the countries
   of the world.

2. The treaty written by the North Atlantic Treaty Organization (NATO)
   is an agreement _____ various Western powers.

3. It was signed during the cold war _____ the East and the West.

4. Trade _____ the United States and Mexico has been increasing.

5. The United States wants to increase trade _____ all countries
   of North America and South America.

107. Beside and Besides, In and Into

> *Beside* means "at the side of" or "next to."
> *Besides* means "in addition to" or "except."
>
> **The driver stood beside his car.**
> **Seven students <u>besides</u> me are in the tennis class.**
>
> Use *in* to show location within something.
> Use *into* to show motion toward a place or a change of location.
>
> **Rabbits live <u>in</u> burrows.**
> **If a rabbit is surprised, it will run <u>into</u> its burrow.**

A. Circle the correct preposition.

1. The jockey stood (beside besides) her horse, Holly's Hope.

2. There are seven horses in the race (besides beside) Holly's Hope.

3. What kind of ice cream do you like (besides beside) strawberry?

4. I don't like any flavor (beside besides) mint.

5. Our class planted a tree (beside besides) the school building.

6. (Besides Beside) the tree we also hope to buy and plant a rose bush.

7. (Beside Besides) the gorilla the snow leopard is an endangered species.

8. The naturalist sat right (beside besides) the gorilla in the wild.

9. Three students (besides beside) Jeanette are absent today.

10. The girl who sits (besides beside) me is a new student.

B. Circle the correct preposition.

1. The diver put on a wetsuit and jumped (in into) the water.

2. The diver went (into in) a large underwater coral reef.

3. The diver saw many unusual creatures (into in) the reef.

4. Many of the reef's inhabitants live (in into) colorful shells.

5. Small fish swim (into in) crevices in the reef if a predator is near.

6. They will hide (in into) the crevices until the danger is past.

7. The diver shined a light (into in) a crevice.

8. He saw a number of fish (into in) the darkness.

9. A small shark sometimes swims (in into) a coral reef.

10. All the other fish hide (in into) safe places until the shark goes away.

Sentences

108. Prepositions and Adverbs

A preposition shows a relationship between its object and some other word in the sentence. An adverb tells how, when, or where. Many words can be used as prepositions or as adverbs.

PREPOSITION

Help is available to the flood victims <u>through</u> the Red Cross.

ADVERB

Because of the flood, trains could not get <u>through</u>.

A. On the line write **P** if the *italicized* word is a preposition or **A** if it is an adverb.

_____ 1. Please open the door and come *in*.

_____ 2. A large fire was burning *in* the fireplace.

_____ 3. The coffee shop *across* the street opens at 6 a.m.

_____ 4. Our teacher always gets his ideas *across* clearly.

_____ 5. Rex, my dog, is always *near* when I'm home.

_____ 6. Rex's bed is *near* the back door.

_____ 7. Please put that box *down* in the kitchen.

_____ 8. The kitchen is *down* those stairs.

_____ 9. There was helium *inside* the balloon.

_____ 10. On cold days I stay *inside* and work on my computer.

B. Write a sentence, using each adverb and each prepositional phrase.

outside *(adverb)*	1.	_____
outside the door	2.	_____
up *(adverb)*	3.	_____
up the stairs	4.	_____
past *(adverb)*	5.	_____
past the house	6.	_____
through *(adverb)*	7.	_____
through the door	8.	_____
in *(adverb)*	9.	_____
in the garden	10.	_____

Sentences

109. Adjective Phrases

An **adjective phrase** is a prepositional phrase used as an adjective.
I read an article about the environment.

A. Underline each adjective phrase.
Circle the noun each modifies.

1. Bees from Africa, called Africanized bees or killer bees, are invading the Americas.

2. People in Brazil originally brought them to the Western Hemisphere.

3. They wanted an increase in honey production.

4. The spread of the bees is occurring gradually.

5. Areas of Texas, New Mexico, Arizona, and California now have these bees.

6. The bees are fierce defenders of their nests.

7. They will immediately attack any nearby source of movement.

8. Numerous bees might join together and make an attack on a person.

9. One defense against these bees is running for shelter.

10. Pursuit by the bees, however, can continue up to a mile!

B. Rewrite each group of words as an adjective phrase.

Example: arrival time   time of arrival

United States flag   1. _____

children's drawings 2. _____

forest animals   3. _____

wolf's den   4. _____

animal's tracks   5. _____

house plants   6. _____

jungle adventures   7. _____

leopard's spots   8. _____

soccer rules   9. _____

piano keys   10. _____

110. More Adjective Phrases

A. Use the noun at the left to write an adjective phrase to complete each sentence.

distance
1. That mountain _____ is Pike's Peak.

courage
2. The world will always need leaders _____.

Brazil
3. Coffee _____ is shipped to the United States.

ice
4. The sidewalk glistened in its coat _____.

California
5. Film studios _____ are where many movies are made.

intelligence
6. Eleanor Roosevelt was a woman _____.

France
7. The United States asked the government _____ for help.

strength
8. Only a person _____ could move this piano alone.

fear
9. This assignment requires a soldier _____.

Poland
10. The flight _____ took off at 10:00 this morning.

B. Complete each sentence with an adjective phrase.

1. The fire _____ caused a great deal of damage.

2. The cheers _____ filled the theater.

3. Hugh is the best player _____.

4. The president _____ gave a report to Congress.

5. The flowers _____ are beautifully arranged.

6. The road _____ is quite narrow.

7. The door _____ is open.

8. The principal _____ made an announcement.

9. The Bill of Rights guarantees freedom _____.

10. The food _____ was delicious.

Sentences

111. Adverb Phrases

An **adverb phrase** is a prepositional phrase used as an adverb.
The United States and Canada are located <u>in North America</u>.

A. Underline each adverb phrase.

1. Buffalo once roamed over the Great Plains.

2. Corn and wheat grow in the Midwest.

3. The Ohio and Missouri Rivers flow into the Mississippi River.

4. Many large cities lie along these rivers.

5. The eastern rim of the plains is formed by the Appalachian Mountains.

6. Across the plains the Rockies and the Sierra Nevadas form the western boundary.

7. Settlers crossed the Great Plains in covered wagons.

8. They built towns in valleys and along rivers.

9. They often lived in simple log cabins.

10. Pioneers sometimes encountered danger in their new homes.

11. Wolves and bears often lived in nearby forests.

12. Settlers farmed during the summer.

13. In the winter they cleared land.

14. Early settlers built towns across the plains.

15. Look on a map and find these locations.

B. Write sentences, replacing the *italicized* adverb with an adverb phrase.

lived *peacefully*   1. _____

moved *westward*   2. _____

grew *swiftly*   3. _____

drove *carefully*   4. _____

listened *silently*   5. _____

112. More Adverb Phrases

A. Complete each sentence with an adverb phrase.

1. The audience laughed _____.

2. _____ our family visits my grandmother.

3. The airplane landed _____.

4. Can you be ready _____?

5. Yesterday afternoon they played ball _____.

6. Kelly lost her backpack _____.

7. I put the candy _____.

8. Flowers grow _____.

9. I sometimes watch TV _____.

10. He parked the car _____.

11. We ate lunch _____.

12. The teacher collected the papers _____.

13. A fire truck drove up _____.

14. Please put the dishes away _____.

15. Hang your coat _____.

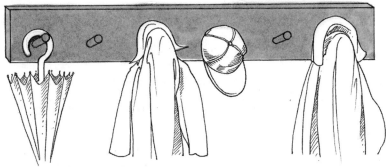

B. Use each adverb phrase in a sentence.

at all times   1. _____

in the park   2. _____

at five o'clock   3. _____

in the living room 4. _____

at school   5. _____

113. Complex Sentences, Adverb Clauses

A **complex sentence** contains an independent clause and one or more dependent clauses. An independent clause has a subject and a verb and can stand alone as a sentence. A dependent clause has a subject and a verb but cannot stand alone as a sentence. A dependent clause usually begins with a **subordinate conjunction,** such as *although, after, because, before, if, provided that, since, so that, unless, until,* or *when.* One type of dependent clause is an **adverb clause.** An adverb clause acts as an adverb and modifies a verb, an adjective, or another adverb.

INDEPENDENT CLAUSE

The Eiffel Tower was the world's tallest structure

DEPENDENT CLAUSE

when it opened in 1889.

A. On the line write **I** if the clause is independent or **D** if it is dependent.

_____ 1. some people thought the tower was an eyesore

_____ 2. because birds might fly into it

_____ 3. although many taller structures have been built

_____ 4. the designer was Alexandre Gustave Eiffel

_____ 5. before the tower was completed

_____ 6. from the top it is possible to see 40 miles in every direction

_____ 7. the two restaurants within the tower offer great views of Paris

_____ 8. unless the day is overcast

_____ 9. while the tower was being constructed

_____ 10. as there is a Web cam on the top of the tower

B. Underline the adverb clause in each sentence. Circle the word(s) it modifies.

1. Before construction of the tower began, people thought it would cost too much.

2. The tower was completed under budget because the crew was so efficient.

3. Although the tower is very tall, it does not sway much in the wind.

4. Eiffel designed the tower so that the wind could blow through it.

5. Since weather erodes the paint, the tower is painted brown every seven years.

6. Until the tower opened, there were few tall structures with elevators.

7. Unless you are prepared to climb about 1,700 steps, you should take an elevator.

8. Because the tower is illuminated, tourists can see its steelwork even at night.

9. Although it is twice as tall as the Washington Monument, it weighs much less.

10. More than 200 million people have visited the tower since it opened.

Sentences

114. Reviewing Sentences

A. Indicate how each *italicized* phrase is used. On the line write **Adj** if it is used as an adjective or **Adv** if it is used as an adverb.

_____ 1. The common cold can be caused *by many different viruses.*

_____ 2. Usually a cold virus is caught *from another person.*

_____ 3. Infections *in the throat* can lead to coughs.

_____ 4. Cough medicine can reduce the amount *of discomfort* a person experiences.

_____ 5. So far no one has invented an actual cure *for the common cold.*

B. Underline each simple subject once. Underline each simple predicate twice. A subject or a predicate may be compound.

6. Microbes grow or multiply on most foods.

7. Is the infection or disease bacterial or viral?

8. The conditions and requirements for their growth vary.

9. Warmth, moisture, and a source of food are necessary to most organisms.

10. In the kitchen, microbes can cause food poisoning.

11. A few steps can reduce or eliminate the chances of poisoning.

12. Meat and poultry should be stored properly and cooked completely.

13. People should refrigerate leftover food promptly.

14. Everyone should wash his or her hands before cooking or eating.

15. People should also wash dishes in hot, soapy water.

C. On the line write **S** if a sentence is simple or **C** if it is compound.

_____ 16. Nutrients give you energy, and they are essential for growth and good health.

_____ 17. Select foods from a variety of food groups.

_____ 18. Fats give your body energy, but protein builds and repairs.

_____ 19. Oranges and grapefruit are excellent sources of vitamin C.

_____ 20. Milk and milk products such as yogurt and cheese supply calcium, protein, and several vitamins.

CONTINUED

Sentences

D. On the line write **N** if the sentence is in natural order or **I** if it is in inverted order. Then rewrite the sentence to change its order.

_____ 21. Did he hear about the swim meet at the park yesterday?

_____

_____ 22. Children from all over the city competed in the meet.

_____

_____ 23. Awarded the first prize was Elena Hernandez.

_____

_____ 24. Onto the winner's podium stepped a smiling Elena.

_____

_____ 25. Will Elena compete in the citywide meet next month?

_____

_____

Try It Yourself

Write four sentences about your favorite book or folktale.
Be sure to use various types of phrases, clauses, and sentences correctly.

_____

_____

_____

_____

Check Your Own Work

Choose a selection from your writing portfolio, your journal,
a work in progress, an assignment from another subject, or a letter.
Revise it, applying the skills you have reviewed. This checklist will help you.

✔ Have you chosen adjective and adverb phrases that add detail to your descriptions?

✔ Have you corrected any incomplete sentences?

✔ Have you used conjunctions, commas, and semicolons correctly to join compound sentences?

Name _____

115. Conjunctions Connecting Words

A **conjunction** is a word used to connect words, phrases, or clauses in a sentence. A **coordinating conjunction** connects similar words or groups of words; it connects words that have the same use in a sentence. These words may be nouns, verbs, adjectives, or adverbs. The coordinating conjunctions are *and, but, or, nor,* and *yet.*

Canadians can watch U.S. TV shows or Canadian TV shows. *(nouns)*
Canada is large but relatively sparse in population. *(adjectives)*
The Canadian hockey team skated quickly and expertly. *(adverbs)*

A. Circle each conjunction. Underline the words it connects.

1. Two of Canada's most important industries are mining and manufacturing.

2. Lakes and streams are abundant in northwestern Canada.

3. Manitoba and Ontario are two Canadian provinces.

4. In parts of Canada you may hear English or French spoken.

5. Many Canadians' first language is not English but French.

6. A passport or proof of U.S. citizenship is required for people traveling between Canada and the United States.

7. The Alaska Highway, a 1,523-mile road, connects Dawson Creek in British Columbia and Fairbanks in Alaska.

8. The Great Lakes are in Canada and the United States.

9. Queen Elizabeth II of England is the head of state and monarch of Canada.

10. The preferred term for the Native Americans of northern Canada is not Eskimo but Inuit.

B. Complete each sentence with words connected by the conjunction.

1. _____ and _____ are states that border my state.

2. My favorite subjects in school are _____ and _____.

3. Today I feel _____ but _____.

4. Tonight I may watch _____ or _____ on TV.

5. My favorite foods are _____ and _____.

116. Conjunctions Connecting Prepositional Phrases

> Coordinating conjunctions can connect prepositional phrases.
> **Many different holidays are celebrated <u>with fireworks</u> and <u>with parades</u>.**

A. Circle each conjunction. Underline the phrases it connects.

1. On July 14, Bastille Day is celebrated in France and in its territories.
2. France's independence day is celebrated with dancing and with fireworks.
3. Soldiers on foot and in military vehicles parade down Paris streets.
4. Dragon Boat Festival in China is also known as Fifth Moon Festival or as Upright Sun Festival.
5. People race long boats with dragon-head fronts and with twisting dragon tails.
6. Cinco de Mayo is celebrated in Mexico and in many U.S. communities.
7. It marks Mexico's victory over the French and over France's colonial ambitions.
8. Street fairs with parades and with folk dancing are held throughout Mexico.
9. Citizenship Day on September 17 gives honor to native U.S. citizens and to naturalized citizens.
10. On September 28 Confucius's birthday is celebrated in China and by Confucius's followers elsewhere.
11. Lectures on his philosophy and about his life are presented.
12. On Earth Day, in April, people learn about the environment and about pollution.
13. People ride to work or to school on bicycles.
14. They are urged to think about conservation and about recycling.
15. Information on commemorative days is available on the Internet and from print sources such as books and magazines.

B. Write sentences with the following prepositional phrases.

1. with music and with dances

   _____

2. on the street and in the home

   _____

3. in Mexico and in the United States

   _____

4. during the afternoon and at night

   _____

5. with special foods and with gifts

   _____

117. Conjunctions Connecting Clauses

Coordinating conjunctions can connect independent clauses or dependent clauses. When a coordinating conjunction joins independent clauses, a comma is used before the conjunction.

Most crocodiles live in fresh water, but some crocodiles live in salt water.

A. Circle each conjunction.
Underline the clauses it connects.

1. Crocodiles are in a group called crocodilians, and alligators belong to the same group.

2. Crocodiles have a protruding tooth, but alligators do not have one.

3. The snout of an alligator is broad, but the snout of a crocodile is narrow.

4. Both animals live in the southeastern part of the United States, and they are found in swamps and on river banks.

5. Alligators rest during the day, and they hunt at night.

6. They may float below the surface, or they may rest in a hole on a bank.

7. Crocodiles eat small aquatic animals, but they sometimes attack large mammals.

8. Alligators usually do not attack humans except in self-defense, but large crocodiles have been known to try to eat humans.

9. Alligators were in danger of extinction, but now laws protect them.

10. Alligators have been saved from extinction, and their numbers have increased.

B. Combine each pair of sentences with an appropriate coordinating conjunction.

1. Alligators live in the Southeast. They don't live in the West.

   _____

2. Alligators were hunted for their skins. The skins were used for clothing.

   _____

3. People tried to save the alligators. Their efforts were successful.

   _____

4. Laws were passed to limit hunting. These laws were effective.

   _____

5. Some people are afraid of alligators. Alligators seldom attack humans.

   _____

118. Reviewing Conjunctions

Underline each conjunction. Write on the line whether it connects words, phrases, or clauses.

_____ 1. Edward played and sang.

_____ 2. Seeds are sown by hand or by machine.

_____ 3. You can take the bus, or you can take the train.

_____ 4. The coldest months are January and February.

_____ 5. Lewis and Clark explored the western United States.

_____ 6. Gloria bought the candy, but Ken ate it.

_____ 7. My mother speaks English and Spanish fluently.

_____ 8. The fox ran under the hedge and into the field.

_____ 9. Maryland and Virginia gave land for the U.S. capital.

_____ 10. These houses are for sale or for rent.

_____ 11. The morning was rainy, but the afternoon was sunny.

_____ 12. Broccoli and cauliflower are delicious.

_____ 13. He ate one sundae, and he ordered another one.

_____ 14. The jelly is on the table or in the refrigerator.

_____ 15. Some airlines offer music and movies.

_____ 16. Kate made a skirt, and Elaine knitted a sweater.

_____ 17. Norway and Sweden are alike in several ways.

_____ 18. Peter shook the tree, and an apple fell to the ground.

_____ 19. Take the expressway, and you will arrive sooner.

_____ 20. Skiing and snowboarding are winter sports.

119. Interjections

An **interjection** is a word that expresses a strong or sudden emotion. Interjections may express happiness, disgust, pain, agreement, impatience, surprise, sadness, amazement, and so on.

<u>Oh, no!</u> The baby spilled a whole box of cereal on the floor!
<u>Wow!</u> Tito Lopez is performing in our town this week.

Underline the interjections. Write on the line what feeling or emotion each interjection expresses.

_____ 1. Look! It's a family of bears.

_____ 2. He likes to eat fried pickles. Gross!

_____ 3. Oh, no! The test is today.

_____ 4. Hush! The president is about to speak!

_____ 5. Good! That was a great answer!

_____ 6. Today is Friday! Hooray!

_____ 7. You have a new cell phone? Great!

_____ 8. Oops! I dropped my sandwich.

_____ 9. Ouch! That plate is hot.

_____ 10. Oh! So that's how you turn on this computer.

_____ 11. Wow! That shirt is really expensive.

_____ 12. Oh, dear! It's raining cats and dogs, and I forgot my umbrella again.

_____ 13. We're having pizza for lunch. Yum!

_____ 14. Yes! Our team won the city championship.

_____ 15. Wonderful! We're going to the mall this afternoon.

_____ 16. Hey! Put that back.

_____ 17. No! You can't be serious.

_____ 18. Pavarotti sings on this CD. Excellent! I love his voice.

_____ 19. Oh, my! That sure costs a lot of money.

_____ 20. You'll be receiving a scholarship. How great!

120. Parts of Speech—Part I

On the line describe each *italicized* word as a noun, pronoun, verb, adjective, adverb, preposition, conjunction, or interjection.

_____ 1. Eleanor Roosevelt *was* one of the most admired and influential first ladies of the United States.

_____ 2. She was born into a *wealthy* New York family that placed great value on education and public service.

_____ 3. She studied in England and later worked *hard* as a teacher in a welfare center on New York's Lower East Side.

_____ 4. In 1905 she married Franklin Roosevelt *and* helped him in his career as a New York politician.

_____ 5. Her husband became *governor* of New York.

_____ 6. After Franklin Roosevelt became president of the United States, she took a *very* active role.

_____ 7. The country was suffering *from* the effects of the Great Depression of 1929, and many people were out of work.

_____ 8. Living conditions for many Americans were *difficult*.

_____ 9. Mrs. Roosevelt visited the poor *and* reported on conditions to her husband.

_____ 10. *She* visited miners, farmers, and factory workers in every part of the country.

_____ 11. She also worked hard to win *equal* rights for women and minorities.

_____ 12. For example, Marian Anderson, an African American opera singer, was *not* allowed to sing in a Washington, D.C., concert hall.

_____ 13. Mrs. Roosevelt organized a concert for *her* at the Lincoln Memorial.

_____ 14. After President Roosevelt died in office in 1945, President Harry S Truman named Mrs. Roosevelt the U.S. *representative* to the United Nations.

_____ 15. She continued to work for human rights until her death in 1962. *Wonderful!*

Eleanor Roosevelt believed in service to the community. What organizations help people in your community? Give an example of something you can do to help them.

Conjunctions, Interjections, Punctuation, Capitalization

121. Parts of Speech—Part II

A. Circle the correct choice in parentheses for each *italized* word.

1. Who killed *President Lincoln?*   (subject direct object)

2. John Wilkes Booth *shot* him in 1865.   (past tense past perfect tense)

3. Booth *was* an actor from the South.   (transitive linking)

4. He was angry about the Civil War, *and* he hated Lincoln.   (conjunction preposition)

5. He found out that Lincoln *might* attend the theater that night.   (auxiliary transitive)

6. Lincoln admired a famous *actress* in the play.   (direct object object complement)

7. The play was *quite* funny.   (degree manner)

8. *Suddenly* a shot rang out.   (adverb adjective)

9. Booth escaped, but *he* hurt his leg.   (third person first person)

10. Lincoln died the day *after* he was shot.   (preposition conjunction)

B. On the line supply the information about the *italicized* word(s).

1. *Who* is this book about?   kind of pronoun   _____

2. *This* book is about Lincoln.   kind of adjective   _____

3. I *will read* it tonight.   tense of verb   _____

4. *He* was the 16th president of the United States.   person of pronoun   _____

5. It was *not* an easy time to be president.   kind of adverb   _____

6. A *fierce* Civil War broke out over slavery.   part of speech   _____

7. The North *and* the South went to war in 1861.   part of speech   _____

8. The Northern army finally *won*.   tense of verb   _____

9. *Alas!* Lincoln did not live to rebuild the country.   part of speech   _____

10. He died *from* an assassin's bullet.   part of speech   _____

122. Periods

A **period** is used at the end of a declarative or an imperative sentence. Periods are also used after many common abbreviations.

> **Gen. D. D. Eisenhower became president and was inaugurated on Jan. 20, 1953.**
> **Please deliver 2 gal. of white paint to 647 S. Prairie Ave. at 8 a.m. on Sat., May 3.**

Periods are not used in abbreviations for metric measures or after the postal abbreviations for states.

> **cm = centimeter   MI = Michigan**

Add periods where needed in these sentences.

1. Rev Conklin asked Prof Angela B Kingston to speak at the awards luncheon

2. The ceremony will take place at 1 pm on Sun, Sept 17

3. Please meet in front of the Miller Bldg at 590 Bell St at 11:30 am

4. Dr Mendoza will pass out the tickets and table assignments then

5. Everyone from R F Kennedy School should attend

6. My cousin C J gave me a great recipe for fruit smoothies

7. Wash 1½ c of your favorite berries and peel 1 small banana

8. Put the fruit in a blender with ½ c yogurt and 4 oz milk

9. Add 6 ice cubes and blend until smooth

10. Enjoy your frosty treat

11. The F W Williams Container Co is located in Beloit, WI

12. They produce 1-gal pails for the Primer Paint Corp and other industries

13. The president of the company is Mrs Sylvia Bache

14. She was recently named Employer of the Year by Gov Stephens

15. Mr Bache and their children are proud of her

16. To get to the zoo, take the No 9 bus about ¾ mi south to the Fullerton Ave stop

17. Catch the No 16 bus and go east about 2 mi to the W Sheridan Rd stop

18. Cross the street and walk about 50 yd south

19. I'll meet you Sat at 2 pm near the zoo entrance

20. Let me know by Fri if you can come

123. Commas in Series, Dates, and Addresses

> **Commas** are used to separate words or groups of words in a series of three or more and to set off parts of dates, addresses, and geographic names.
>
> **Illinois produces corn, soybeans, and wheat.**
>
> **Springfield, Illinois, was Lincoln's home for many years.**
>
> **Illinois joined the Union on December 3, 1818, as the 21st state.**
>
> **The John Hancock Building, once the tallest apartment building in the world, is located at 875 North Michigan Avenue, Chicago, Illinois 60611.**

A. Insert commas where needed.

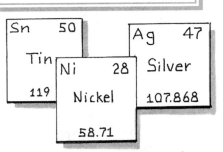

1. Silver mercury tin and nickel are metals.
2. These metals are found in the United States South Africa and Canada.
3. Coal oil and natural gas are fossil fuels.
4. The United States imports petroleum from Canada Saudi Arabia and Mexico.
5. Acid rain from the burning of fossil fuels harms plants animals and people.
6. Fossil fuels are obtained by drilling strip-mining and tunneling.
7. The United States should explore alternative kinds of energy, such as solar power wind power and nuclear power.
8. Geysers volcanoes and tides are other natural sources of energy.
9. A fuel called methanol can be obtained from wood coal and natural gas.
10. In the meantime people mine coal dig oil wells and tap natural gas.

B. Rewrite the sentences, inserting commas where needed.

1. The United States adopted the Constitution on September 17 1787.

   _____

2. Philadelphia Pennsylvania is where the Constitution was written.

   _____

3. Boonesboro Kentucky reportedly was founded by Daniel Boone on April 1 1775.

   _____

4. The White House is at 1600 Pennsylvania Avenue Washington D.C.

   _____

5. The *Mayflower* landed at what is now Plymouth Massachusetts on December 21 1620.

   _____

124. Commas in Letters and with Appositives

Commas are used after the salutation in both social and friendly letters and after the closing in all letters.

> **Dear Aunt Helen,**   *(after salutation)*
>
>   **Thanks for the video games you gave me for my birthday. I play them every day after I finish my homework.**
>
>   **Love,**   *(after closing)*
>   **Bradley**

Commas are used to set off nonrestrictive appositives.

> **William the Conqueror, the first Norman king of England, gained control of England in 1066.**

A. Insert commas where needed.

> **Dear Aunt Marge and Uncle Ralph**
>
>   **Thanks for taking Billy and me camping last week. It was really fun to visit Yellowstone Park and see the bears and geysers. I hope you can spend Christmas with us again this year.**
>
>   **Love**
>   **Paula**

B. Insert commas where needed.

1. Queen Elizabeth II the present queen of England ascended the throne on February 6, 1952.

2. The queen's father George VI had been king from 1936 to 1952.

3. George VI became king when one of his brothers Edward VIII abdicated in order to marry Wallis Simpson an American woman.

4. George VI and Elizabeth his wife courageously stayed in London during the bombings of World War II.

5. Queen Elizabeth II is married to Phillip Mountbatten the Duke of Edinburgh.

6. Prince Charles her eldest son is next in line to the throne.

7. Prince Charles has two sons Prince William and Prince Henry.

8. Diana the Princess of Wales died in a tragic automobile accident in Paris in 1997.

9. The elder son of Charles and Diana Prince William is second in line for the throne.

10. Over the years some people have wondered whether the English monarchy might end upon the death of the present sovereign Queen Elizabeth II.

125. Commas with Quotations

Commas are used to set off short direct quotations from the rest of the sentence. If the quotation is at the beginning of the sentence, place a comma after the last word of the quotation, unless a question mark or an exclamation point is needed.

"Mexico is the United States' neighbor to the south," said Professor Louis.

If the quotation is at the end of the sentence, place a comma after the last word before the quotation.

Professor Louis said, "Mexico is the United States' neighbor to the south."

If the quotation is divided, use a comma after the first part and before the latter part.

"Mexico," Professor Louis said, "is the United States' neighbor to the south."

Insert commas where needed. Not every sentence needs a comma.

1. "Mexico" said Professor Louis "has a long and rich history."

2. "The original inhabitants of Mexico were Native Americans of various groups, including the Aztecs and the Toltecs" he said.

3. "These indigenous groups built important civilizations" he continued.

4. A student asked "What happened to those civilizations?"

5. "They changed dramatically" he answered "when the Spanish arrived, starting in 1492."

6. He stated "By 1535 Mexico was completely under Spanish control."

7. "During the colonial period many indigenous achievements were forgotten or lost" he said.

8. "What a terrible thing!" a student exclaimed.

9. The professor told the students "Mexico declared its independence from Spain in 1810."

10. "However" he continued "Spain did not recognize Mexico's independence until 1821."

11. "Mexico had several forms of government" he explained "in the following years, including a republic and an empire."

12. One student asked "What is Mexico like today?"

13. "Nowadays" said the professor "Mexico is a developing country with deep cultural traditions."

14. "Mexico is rich in mineral wealth, and it is an important manufacturing center" he said.

15. "Tourism is an important business as well" concluded the professor.

126. Commas in Compound Sentences

A comma is used to separate the clauses of a compound sentence connected by the coordinating conjunction *and, but, or, nor,* or *yet.*

The Atlantic Ocean is east of the United States, and the Pacific Ocean is west.

A. Insert commas where needed. If no comma is needed, write **NC** on the line.

_____ 1. The longest river in the United States is the Missouri but the Nile River is longer.

_____ 2. The Great Lakes compose the world's largest freshwater system and the Mississippi River is the longest river that flows southward.

_____ 3. The rivers of Japan are short but many have waterfalls.

_____ 4. The most important rivers in northern Europe are the Danube and the Rhine.

_____ 5. The Amazon River is the longest river in South America and the Paraná is the second-longest.

_____ 6. The Congo River is the longest river in sub-Saharan Africa but the Nile River in Egypt is longer.

_____ 7. The Yangtze River is the longest river in China and in all of Asia.

_____ 8. People use rivers to generate electricity and they also use them as a means of transportation.

_____ 9. Rivers are a source of water for drinking and for the irrigation of crops.

_____ 10. This summer I will sail the Mississippi River or I will take a cruise on the Amazon.

B. Complete each sentence with a coordinating conjunction and a comma if required.

1. Root beer was a type of herbal tea _____ later it became a soft drink.

2. In England some people eat eggs _____ drink tea for breakfast.

3. Natural spring water is bottled at a spring _____ it is prized for its mineral content.

4. The syrup for colas was first created as a cure for headaches _____ now people drink colas anytime.

5. Carbonated drinks first came only in bottles _____ later they became available in cans.

Name _____

127. Reviewing Commas

Insert commas where needed.

1. The European Renaissance started in Italy and it spread to all the other countries of Europe.

2. The Renaissance a reawakening of learning started in about 1350.

3. During the Renaissance scholars rediscovered classical Greek and Roman writings and they studied the ancient texts earnestly.

4. Painting sculpture and architecture began to change at this time too.

5. Three centers of activity were Rome Florence and Venice.

6. In Florence a city in central Italy the members of the ruling family were patrons of the arts.

7. The patrons members of the Medici family supported many important artists.

8. One of these artists was Michelangelo a noted painter and sculptor.

9. Michelangelo created beautiful sculptures for the city of Florence and he created wonderful paintings in Rome.

10. Michelangelo died on February 18 1564.

11. One person said "The world has many kings but only one Michelangelo."

12. Other important Renaissance artists are Leonardo da Vinci Sandro Botticelli and Raphael.

13. They painted religious subjects figures from ancient myths and portraits of contemporary people.

14. Museums around the world exhibit many Renaissance works and these are greatly admired today.

15. The Renaissance profoundly influenced art music and thought.

16. Bob asked "Have you read the history of the Renaissance?"

17. "Yes" Pam answered "the Renaissance was the topic of my last report."

18. "The Renaissance" our teacher said "is an extremely important period in European history."

19. The *Mona Lisa* da Vinci's most famous painting can be seen in the Louvre Museum.

20. You can get information on Italy by writing to the Italian Government Travel Office at 630 Fifth Avenue New York NY 10111.

Name _____

128. Exclamation Points and Question Marks

An **exclamation point** is used at the end of an exclamatory sentence to express a strong emotion or reaction. An exclamation point is also used after an interjection or exclamatory words to express happiness, disgust, pain, agreement, impatience, surprise, sadness, amazement, or other strong emotion.

What a great gymnast he is!
Oh, no! He fell off the parallel bars.

A **question mark** is used at the end of a question.

Who do you think will win the event?

A. Add an exclamation point or a question mark where needed.

1. Shh Did you hear that noise
2. What a great movie that was
3. We won the game Hooray
4. When will you bake the brownies
5. Hurry up Don't you want to be on time
6. Will you babysit tonight Great
7. Who made these delicious cookies
8. How lucky you were
9. Where are the baby's toys
10. Quick Run inside

B. Add a period, an exclamation point, or a question mark where needed.

1. What is a peninsula
2. Spain, Italy, and Greece are located on peninsulas
3. What is the difference between a peninsula and an island
4. Which state in the United States is made up of a group of islands
5. Wow It's really far away from the mainland
6. Alaska has a group of islands too
7. Several places on the coast of South Carolina become islands when the tide is high
8. When the tide is low, they are connected to the mainland by sandbars
9. No kidding Can you drive to those islands
10. Many of the sandbars are quite compact, and a small car can drive on them

129. Semicolons

> A **semicolon** is used to separate the clauses of a compound sentence when they are not separated by a coordinating conjunction such as *and, but,* or *or.* Semicolons are also used to separate items in a series when the items themselves contain commas.
>
> **I have read a lot about South America; it has an interesting history.**
> **I have been to Buenos Aires, Argentina; Santiago, Chile; and**
> **Montevideo, Uruguay.**

A. Rewrite each sentence. Replace the comma and the coordinating conjunction with a semicolon.

1. Simón Bolívar was born in South America, and he was the son of an aristocrat.

   _____

2. In 1810 Bolívar joined a revolt against Spain, but his forces were defeated.

   _____

3. Bolívar led another revolt in 1817, and this time he liberated Venezuela.

   _____

4. Bolívar fought other battles, and he helped liberate Colombia, Ecuador, and Peru.

   _____

5. Bolívar is remembered as a great hero, and his birthday is a national holiday in Venezuela and Bolivia.

   _____

   _____

B. Insert commas and semicolons where necessary.

1. They visited Rome Italy Paris France and London England.

2. Bolívar won battles on June 24 1821 May 3 1822 and August 6 1825.

3. I thanked Mrs. Cabot my principal Ms. Caputo my teacher and Mr. Bendix my coach.

4. The teams in the North Division are located in Green Bay Wisconsin Chicago Illinois Detroit Michigan and Minneapolis Minnesota.

5. My brothers were born on February 3 1999 April 16 2001 and October 30 2003.

Conjunctions, Interjections, Punctuation, Capitalization

130. Colons

A **colon** is used after the salutation of a business letter.

> **Dear Dr. Bradley:**

A colon is also used before a list of items. A colon must never follow a verb.

> **You will need these items: wood glue, a screwdriver, and a vise.**
> **You can make a bookcase, a shoe rack, or a step stool.**

Decide whether each sentence needs a colon. If it does, rewrite the sentence, adding the colon in the correct place.

1. We are learning about the following three types of cephalopods octopuses, squids, and cuttlefish.

   _____

   _____

2. Cephalopods are related to these bivalves that you may have eaten scallops, oysters, and clams.

   _____

3. Cephalopods are found in oceans all over the world in the tropics, at the poles, along the shore, and in the open sea.

   _____

   _____

4. These animals can change their colors, their shapes, and their body textures.

   _____

5. They appeared on earth long ago before mammals, before vertebrates, even before most kinds of plants.

   _____

   _____

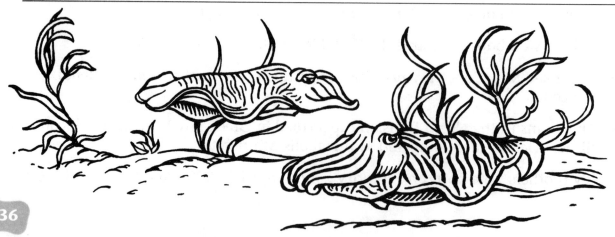

131. Quotation Marks

> **Quotation marks** are placed before and after every complete quotation and every part of a divided quotation. Commas and periods go inside the quotation marks. A question mark or an exclamation point goes inside the quotation marks if it is part of the quotation but outside the quotation marks if it is part of the entire sentence.
>
> **"I'm sorry," said Jake, "but I'm going to be late."**
> **"Can I help you?" asked Marty.   Who said, "The game is over"?**
>
> Quotation marks are used to set off the titles of songs, short stories, poems, magazine articles, newspaper articles, and episodes of television series. Titles of books, magazines, newspapers, movies, plays, operas, TV series, and works of art are printed in italic type. When these titles are handwritten, they are underlined.
>
> **I read "How to Save the Planet" in *Time* magazine.** (printed title, italic type)
> **He sang "Now" on the TV series <u>Kids</u>.** (handwritten title, underlined)

Rewrite each sentence, adding quotation marks and underlining where needed.

1. Jack Prelutsky's poem The Crocodile appeared in the book Zoo Doings.

   _____

2. Is The March of the Penguins a good movie? Gracie asked.

   _____

3. She played the song Octopus's Garden from the album Abbey Road.

   _____

4. I didn't know, Tim remarked, that she likes the Beatles.

   _____

5. The Golden Book of Fairy Tales includes the story The Frog Prince.

   _____

6. Who read the Chicago Tribune article Walrus Fans Sure to Blubber with Joy?

   _____

7. Rick said My little brother's favorite book is Where the Wild Things Are.

   _____

8. Oh! exclaimed Andy. That was my favorite book too.

   _____

9. Tonight's episode of the TV show Champions of the Wild is called Manatee.

   _____

10. In the book The Old Man and the Sea, Santiago struggles to catch a giant fish.

   _____

132. Apostrophes

An **apostrophe** is used to show possession; to show the omission of a letter, letters, or numbers; and to show the plural of a small letter.

> **Brad's report is on Jesse Owens's performance at the '36 Olympic games.**
> **The women's book group and the boys' scout troop both meet today.**
> **Don't forget that Mississippi has two *p*'s, four *i*'s, and four *s*'s.**

An apostrophe is not used to form the plural of a number or of an abbreviation that does not have periods. Also, an apostrophe is not used to form the plural of a capital letter unless the plural form can be misread,

> **10s   1940s   URLs   Rs (but I's)**

Insert apostrophes where needed.

1. I enjoy Emily Dickinsons poetry.

2. The painting *The Spirit of 76* is by Archibald M. Willard.

3. He recited Longfellows poem "Paul Reveres Ride."

4. Edgar Allan Poes middle name is spelled with two *as*.

5. I cant remember C. S. Lewiss first name.

6. The moons orbit around Earth takes about 30 days.

7. The blizzard of 01 is one of this centurys storms that weve read about.

8. Hes visiting the Zócolo, Mexico Citys main plaza.

9. Susan has difficulty writing *rs* and *zs* correctly.

10. The Joneses house was built in the 1970s.

11. Ill open Granddads present first.

12. Please dont touch Carloss toys.

13. He didnt write the boys last names in alphabetical order.

14. My mom couldnt believe that I got all As on my report card.

15. Theyve provided the uniforms for all the girls soccer teams.

16. Atlantas Summer Olympic Games were in 96.

17. Jens and Rhondas entries won top prizes.

18. The ascenders on your *bs* and *hs* shouldnt touch the letters above them.

19. Andrew Wyeths most famous painting is called *Christinas World*.

20. She hasnt read Laura Rubys book *Lilys Ghosts*.

133. Hyphens

> A **hyphen** is used to divide a word at the end of a line when one or more syllables are carried to the next line. It is also used in some compound words and in the numbers from twenty-one to ninety-nine when these numbers are written out.
>
> **My brother-in-law put himself through college and grad-uated when he was only twenty-eight.**
>
> Some compounds are hyphenated only when they act as adjectives.
>
> **I like ice cream, so I bought an ice-cream cone.**

A. Add hyphens to the compounds that normally use them. Check a dictionary if you need help.

1. self respect
2. attorney general
3. off line
4. dirt bike
5. sister in law

6. blue jay
7. old fashioned
8. saber toothed
9. line drive
10. parking lot

B. Add hyphens where necessary. Check a dictionary if you need help.

1. My cousin's father in law took his eight year old neighbor to the circus, where they saw an amazing high wire act.

2. In case of an emergency, pack your car with a first aid kit, a blanket, a good flash light, and some bottled water.

3. I saw a ruby throated hummingbird among the forget me nots in grand mother's garden.

4. A month may contain twenty eight, twenty nine, thirty, or thirty one days.

5. The thyroid, a butterfly shaped gland located in the throat, controls the body's metabolism and energy level.

6. Niagara Falls consists of three fast flowing waterfalls that lie on the border be tween Canada and the United States.

7. The happy go lucky boy ate at a fast food restaurant and then walked aim lessly around town.

8. A mountain lion is a large, powerfully built wildcat that is found in the moun tainous regions of northwest North America.

9. Romeo and Juliet, Shakespeare's star crossed lovers, die because of their mis understandings.

10. All twenty two members of Mr. Spivak's eighth grade class chipped in to get him a retirement gift.

134. Capital Letters

Use **capital letters** in these places:

THE FIRST WORD IN A SENTENCE	Help is on its way.
THE FIRST WORD OF A DIRECT QUOTATION	Patrick Henry said, "Give me liberty or give me death!"
PROPER NOUNS AND ADJECTIVES	I went to France last year. Let's buy some Colombian coffee.
TITLES BEFORE A NAME	Let's ask Reverend Washington.
NORTH, SOUTH, EAST, AND WEST WHEN THEY REFER TO SECTIONS OF THE COUNTRY	The South lost the Civil War.
ALL NAMES REFERRING TO DEITIES	The Arabic word for God is *Allah*.
THE BIBLE OR PARTS OF THE BIBLE, AND OTHER SACRED WORKS	The creation story is in Genesis.
THE PRINCIPAL WORDS IN TITLES	Let's watch *Gone with the Wind*.
THE PRONOUN *I*	Phil and I walked home together.
ABBREVIATIONS WHEN CAPITALS WOULD BE USED IF THE WORDS WERE WRITTEN IN FULL	He is Dr. Ahkook Sawlani, M.D.
THE FIRST WORD OF EVERY LINE OF MOST POETRY	Lift ev'ry voice and sing, Till earth and heaven ring . . .

Use the proofreading symbol (≡) under the letters that should be capitalized.

1. louise remarked, "there is a special message about thanksgiving on the bulletin board."

2. the most important leader of the civil rights movement was dr. martin luther king, jr.

3. petra recited langston hughes's "life is fine," and i recited "harlem."

4. the bible, the koran, and the torah are all important sacred works.

5. fred asked, "have you ever been to the smithsonian institution?"

6. *honey, i shrunk the kids* is a really funny movie.

7. my dentist is dr. ron oakdale, d.d.s.

8. the robbery case was tried before judge amos abraham.

9. the west attracted many settlers in the 1800s.

10. pike's peak is in colorado.

135. Reviewing Punctuation and Capitalization

A. Write the correct punctuation mark in each box.
On the line write which punctuation mark or marks you used.

Across

_____ 3. What☐s the longest river in the world?

_____ 4. Great☐ The Nile is the right answer.

_____ 5. The address of the wildlife organization is
70 E. Falmouth Highway☐ East Falmouth, MA 02536.

_____ 6. There are many endangered species☐ rhinoceroses, **pandas**,
and tigers.

_____ 7. Anita asked☐ "Do you know who wrote *The Adventures of
Tom Sawyer?*"

_____ 8. It☐s one of Mark Twain's best-loved works.

Down

_____ 1. "Where is Puget Sound☐" asked Nancy.

_____ 2. We learned about Washington state☐ its natural **resources**,
its history, and its current econmy.

_____ 5. We went to the top of the Empire State Building☐ took a
boat to the Statue of Liberty☐ and shopped on **Fifth Avenue**.

_____ 6. Rockefeller Center is located in New York☐ New York.

B. Use the names of the punctuation marks
in Part A to complete the crossword puzzle.

C. Rewrite each sentence with correct punctuation and capitalization.

11. the abbreviation j.f.k. in our librarys name stands for john fitzgerald kennedy

_____

_____

12. annually the american library association awards the john newbery medal to
    an outstanding childrens book

_____

_____

13. no I havent read the latest winner

_____

14. in canada the canadian library association awards a similar prize to a canadian book

_____

_____

15. do you enjoy reading science fiction fantasy or nonfiction

_____

Try It Yourself

Write four sentences about what you studied in school this week.
Be sure to use punctuation and capitalization correctly.

_____

_____

_____

_____

Check Your Own Work

Choose a selection from your writing portfolio, your journal, a work in progress,
an assignment from another subject, or a letter. Revise it, applying the skills you
have reviewed. This checklist will help you.

✔ Have you followed the rules for commas?

✔ Have you used quotation marks with direct quotations
   and around titles of short works?

✔ Have you followed the rules for capitalization?

✔ Do your sentences end with correct punctuation marks?

136. Subjects and Predicates

A **diagram** is a picture of a sentence. It shows how the words in a sentence relate to each other. A diagram highlights the most important words and clearly indicates the words that go with them.

Start the diagram by drawing a horizontal line. Find the verb in the sentence and write it on the right half of the horizontal line. Find the subject. Write it to the left of the verb. Separate the subject and the verb by a vertical line that cuts through the horizontal line.

A word that describes the subject or the verb is written on a slanting line under the subject or the verb.

SENTENCE: **The graceful swallows flew swiftly.**

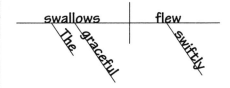

Diagram each sentence.

1. The unhappy baby wailed loudly.

2. The orange cat is sleeping.

3. The hungry children ate quickly.

CONTINUED

4. The contest will end tomorrow.

5. The black clouds were approaching rapidly.

6. The lead guitarist sings well.

7. The carefree boy whistled happily.

8. The little brown puppy barked excitedly.

Name _____

137. Direct Objects and Indirect Objects

In a diagram a direct object is written on the main horizontal line to the right of the verb. It is separated from the verb by a vertical line that touches the horizontal line but does not cut through it.

An indirect object is placed on a horizontal line under the verb and is connected to the verb by a slanting line.

SENTENCE: **The boy gave his mother the large package.**

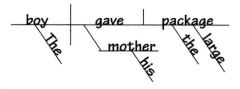

Diagram each sentence.

1. The principal will award the top students prizes.

2. Kate sent her uncle a thank-you note.

3. This online catalog guarantees its customers prompt delivery.

CONTINUED

Diagramming

4. The cheerful babysitter is teaching the children a new game.

5. Marcus showed me his secret hideout.

6. My cousin lent my big brother his new car.

7. The teacher assigned the noisy students extra homework.

8. Randy's energetic spaniel often chases squirrels.

9. A local citizen wrote the governor a long letter.

138. Subject Complements

In a diagram a subject complement is written to the right of the verb on the main horizontal line. It is separated from the verb by a slanted line that points back toward the subject. The slanted line touches the horizontal line but does not cut through it.

SENTENCE: **Harry Potter is my favorite literary character.**

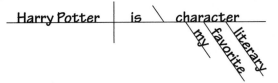

Diagram each sentence.

1. These plates are dirty.

2. The brisk wind felt chilly.

3. Tomorrow will be your lucky day.

4. Abraham Lincoln was very tall.

CONTINUED

Diagramming

5. An okapi is an unusual African mammal.

6. My favorite snack is hot, crunchy popcorn.

7. Those boys look extremely happy.

8. Our class's best speller is she.

9. Mount Rushmore is a popular tourist destination.

10. His choice possession is his new skateboard.

139. Appositives

In a diagram an appositive is placed in parentheses to the right of the word it identifies. Words that describe the appositive go under it.

SENTENCE: **The puffin, an arctic sea bird, eats small fish.**

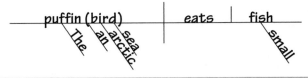

Diagram each sentence.

1. Paul McCartney wrote "Hey Jude," a popular Beatles' song.

2. The American inventor Thomas Edison developed the first phonograph.

3. Mom prepared my favorite dessert, chocolate cake with creamy frosting.

4. Seattle's symbol is the Space Needle, a famous landmark.

CONTINUED

Diagramming

5. My little sister enjoys *Sesame Street,* an excellent children's show.

6. Our block party, an annual celebration, will be held tomorrow.

7. Loretta's parents got her a new pet, a golden hamster.

8. My uncle, an award-winning cook, is also a fine mechanic.

9. I bought my friend a birthday present, a new computer game.

10. George Washington, our first president, was once a surveyor.

140. Intensive Pronouns and Reflexive Pronouns

In a diagram an intensive pronoun is placed in parentheses directly to the right of the word it emphasizes. A reflexive pronoun is placed according to its function in the sentence, as the direct object or the indirect object or as the object of a preposition.

SENTENCE: **I will frost the cookies myself.**   SENTENCE: **She wrote herself a note.**

SENTENCE: **The wrestlers weighed themselves regularly.**

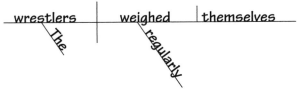

Diagram each sentence.

1. The boys made themselves some hot chocolate.

2. Karen herself cleaned the garage.

3. My little brother cannot feed himself yet.

CONTINUED

Diagramming

4. My cousin rebuilt the engine himself.

5. My mother bought herself a new computer.

6. The old cat slowly stretched itself.

7. Karl will cook the whole meal himself.

8. The bird made itself a cozy nest.

9. The coaches themselves will award the prizes.

141. Prepositional Phrases

In a diagram a prepositional phrase goes under the word it describes. The preposition goes on a slanting line. The object of the preposition goes on a horizontal line connected to the line with the preposition. Any words that describe the object go under it.

SENTENCE: **The man at the podium is speaking about the new gym.**

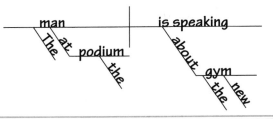

Diagram each sentence.

1. The flowers in the blue vase need water.

2. The cat is sunning itself on the back porch.

3. Martha hid the presents under her bed.

4. I made myself a big pot of tomato soup.

5. The boy with the blue bike is my next-door neighbor.

6. A woman on the bus was carrying a bunch of red balloons.

7. The ball crashed through the garage window.

8. The members of the cleanup committee got coupons for free pizzas.

9. Mrs. Silva, the president of the parents' club, made a special announcement.

142. Compound Sentence Parts

In a diagram compound sentence parts are placed on separate horizontal lines, with the coordinating conjunction on a dashed line between them. The horizontal lines are placed in their correct position in the diagram.

SENTENCE: **Mom and I picked tomatoes and corn and served them for dinner.**

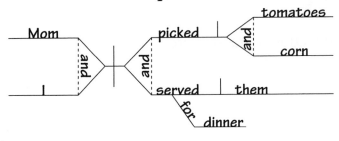

SENTENCE: **My favorite dish is roast chicken and stuffing with onions and sausage.**

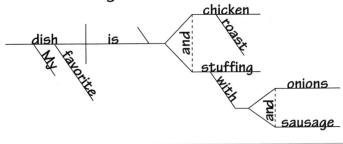

Diagram each sentence.

1. Cockatoos and macaws are kinds of parrots.

2. Tim and Trudy went to the zoo and the aquarium.

3. Benjamin Franklin was a diplomat and an inventor.

CONTINUED

Diagramming

4. My dad and I washed the car and cleaned the garage.

5. The teacher gave Rob and Helen instructions and encouragement.

6. He went to the library and borrowed a book about pandas.

7. My aunt and my uncle bought a boat and sailed to Aruba and Barbados.

8. My grandfather worked hard and became a successful engineer.

143. Compound Sentences

In a diagram each independent clause of a compound sentence is diagrammed separately on its own horizontal line. The coordinating conjunction is placed between the clauses on a dashed vertical line that connects the left edges of horizontal lines.

SENTENCE: **The sky was very cloudy, but we started the game anyway.**

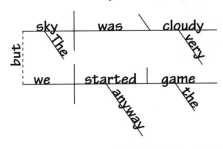

Diagram each sentence.

1. I could not find the information in the library, but I located it online.

2. The party will be held in the gym, and everyone should wear a costume.

3. We can see that movie in the theater, or we can rent the DVD.

CONTINUED

Diagramming

4. Ray did his homework before dinner, but Rita watched TV.

5. An ostrich is a large creature, but it has a small brain.

6. I received the application yesterday, and I completed it immediately.

7. Mia bought Luke a birthday present, and she gave it to him today.

8. You should bring the cushions inside, or the rain will ruin them.

144. Interjections

In a diagram an interjection is placed on a line that is separate from the rest of the sentence. The line is above, to the left, and parallel to the main horizontal line.

SENTENCE: **Help! The rope is breaking!**

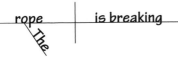

Diagram each sentence.

1. Ah! That breeze feels wonderful.

2. Oh! You startled me.

3. Well! I will never do that again.

4. Sh! We should not spoil the surprise.

5. Hey! You splashed water on me.

6. Good, we finally finished our chores!

7. Oops! My ice cream fell in the sand.

8. Yikes! You are going to be late for practice.

9. Wow! Your new skateboard is great!

10. Gee, that is an enormous fish!

145. Adverb Clauses

In a diagram an adverb clause goes on its own horizontal line under the independent clause. The conjunction is placed on a slanted line that connects the two clauses. The line goes from the verb in the adverb clause to the word in the independent clause that the adverb clause describes, which is usually the verb.

SENTENCE: **After we planted the garden, we had cookies and lemonade.**

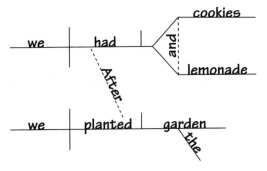

Diagram each sentence.

1. They will not finish the job until they buy more paint.

2. After the settlers crossed the river, they camped for the night.

3. Although the house was attractive, the Smiths did not buy it.

Diagramming

4. John made himself a sandwich before he left for the game.

5. We were late because we had a flat tire.

6. Laura made the toast while Anna scrambled the eggs.

7. When Wes dropped the ball, Jerry scored the final run.

8. The children played tag in the yard until they were called for dinner.

146. Diagramming Review

In a diagram each part of a sentence has its own place.

Diagram each sentence.

1. The boys went into the kitchen and made themselves some lunch.

2. The famous architect Frank Gehry designed the new museum

3. She cannot finish the puzzle unless she finds the lost piece.

4. My brother and I built the birdhouse ourselves, but Dad hung it in the tree.

Diagramming

5. Yikes! The cat is on the roof, and it will not come down.

6. The whole school was proud when the chess team won the tournament.

7. My aunt is an attorney and the author of three law books.

8. Will Frank send Harry an e-mail or will he call him on the phone?

9. Grizzly bears are large and powerful, and they can be very aggressive.

10. William Howard Taft, our 27th president, became Chief Justice of the Supreme Court.

ADJECTIVES

An **adjective** points out or describes a noun.

An **article** points out a noun. *A, an* and *the* are articles. *The* is the **definite article.** *A* and *an* are **indefinite articles:** *The* boy ate *an* apple and *a* pear.

A **demonstrative adjective** points out a specific person, place, or thing. *This, that, these,* and *those* are demonstrative adjectives: *this* book, *those* pencils.

A **descriptive adjective** tells about age, size, shape, color, origin, or another quality of a noun. A descriptive adjective usually comes before the noun it describes. It may also follow a linking verb: It was a *sunny* morning. The popcorn tasted *great.*

An **indefinite adjective** refers to any or all members of a group. Indefinite adjectives include *all, another, any, both, each, either, few, many, more, most, much, neither, other, several,* and *some: both* boys, *either* girl.

An **interrogative adjective** is used in questions. *What, which,* and *whose* are interrogative adjectives: *Whose* book is this?

A **possessive adjective** shows possession or ownership. The possessive adjectives are *my, your* (singular), *his, her, its, our, your* (plural), and *their: my* car, *your* motorcycle: *her* hat, *your* book.

Some adjectives tell exactly how many: *ten, twenty-five, third, twelfth.* Some adjectives tell about how many: *many, few, several, some.*

See also **antecedents, comparisons, prepositions, sentences, subject-verb agreement.**

ADVERBS

An **adverb** modifies a verb, an adjective, or another adverb.

- An **adverb of affirmation** tells that something is positive or gives consent or approval: The music is *certainly* beautiful.

- An **adverb of degree** answers the question how much or how little: The boy is *quite* tall.

- An **adverb of manner** answers the question how, or in what manner: Jason draws *well*.

- An **adverb of negation** expresses a negative condition or refusal: The door is *not* locked.

- An **adverb of place** answers the question where: Sit *here* by the gate.

- An **adverb of time** answers the question when or how often: It rained *yesterday*.

A negative idea is expressed by using one negative word. This negative word may be *no, not, none, never,* or *nothing.* These words should be used only in sentences that have no other negative words: I do not have *any* (not *no*) apples.

See also **clauses, comparisons, prepositions.**

ANTECEDENTS

The noun to which a pronoun or possessive adjective refers is its **antecedent.** A pronoun or a possessive adjective must agree with its antecedent in person and number. A third person singular pronoun or possessive adjective must agree in gender also.

See also **adjectives, pronouns.**

CAPITALIZATION

Capital letters are used for many purposes, including the following:

- The first word of a sentence—The bell rang.

- Proper nouns and proper adjectives—Betsy Ross, American flag

- An abbreviation if the word it stands for begins with a capital letter—Rev. for Reverend

- The first word and the name of a person addressed in the salutation of a letter and the first word in the complementary close of a letter—Dear Marie, Yours truly,

- The principal words in the titles of books, plays, works of art, and poems—*A Tale of Two Cities, Romeo and Juliet, Mona Lisa,* "Fire and Ice"

- The first word of a direct quotation—Mother said, "It's time for my favorite television program."

- Titles when used before a person's name—Thank you, Professor Higgins.

- North, East, South, West when they refer to sections of the country or the world. They are not capitalized when they refer to directions—the old West. He drove west on Main Street.

- The pronoun *I*

- Names referring to deities or sacred works—God, the Bible

- Two-letter state postal abbreviations—MA, NY, CA

- The first word of each line of most poetry

CLAUSES

A **clause** is a group of related words that contains a subject and predicate.

A **dependent clause** does not express a complete thought and cannot stand alone. A dependent clause, together with an independent clause, forms a complex sentence.

- An **adverb clause** is a dependent clause used as an adverb. Adverb clauses are usually introduced by conjunctions such as *although, as, after, because, before, for, since, that, though, unless, until, where,* and *while: After we had canoed down the river,* we went to a clambake on the beach.

An **independent clause** expresses a complete thought. An independent clause can stand alone as a sentence: After we had canoed down the river, *we went to a clambake on the beach.*

See also **sentences.**

COMPARISONS

Many adjectives and adverbs can be used to compare two or more persons, places, things, or actions.

- The **positive degree** describes one or more persons, places, things, or actions: The *tall* boy ran *fast.*

- The **comparative degree** compares two persons, places, things, or actions. Form comparatives by adding *-er* to the positive degree or by putting *more* or *less* before the positive degree: The *younger* child cried *more sadly.*

- The **superlative degree** compares three or more persons, places, things, or actions. Form superlatives by adding *-est* to the positive degree or by putting *most* or *least* before the positive degree: The *tallest* boy ran *most quickly.*

Few, fewer, and *fewest* are used to compare count nouns. *Little, less,* and *least* are used to compare noncount nouns: *little* money, *few* dimes.

CONJUNCTIONS

A conjunction is used to connect words, phrases, or clauses in a sentence.

A **coordinating conjunction** connects similar words, phrases, or clauses. *And, or, but, nor,* and *yet* are coordinating conjunctions: Todd *and* Cindy will come early to help us. They will research on the Internet *and* in the library. We left on time, *but* we got there late.

See also **clauses, sentences.**

CONTRACTIONS

A **contraction** is two words written as one with one or more letters omitted. An apostrophe is used to show the omission of a letter or letters: *we're, she's, don't, I'll.*

INTERJECTIONS

An **interjection** expresses a strong or sudden emotion, such as delight, disgust, pain, agreement, impatience, surprise, sorrow, or wonder: *Oh! Shh! Ouch! Wow!*

MOOD

Mood shows the manner in which an action or state of being is expressed.

- The **indicative mood** of a verb is used to make a statement or ask a question. Most sentences are in the indicative mood: Where *are* you *going?* Tom *is going* to the park.

- The **emphatic form** of the indicative mood gives special force to a simple present or past tense verb. To make an emphatic form, use *do, does,* or *did* before the base form of the verb: I *do want* to go! She *does have* a pony. They *did find* the treasure.

- The **imperative mood** is used to express a command or a request. To form the imperative, use the base form of the verb. The subject of an imperative sentence is understood to be the pronoun *you:* Please open the door. A command can be given in the third person by using *let's* before the base form of a verb: *Let's* measure the rug.

- The **subjunctive mood** is used in several ways: to express a wish or a desire; to express a request, a command, or a suggestion after the word *that;* or to express something that is contrary to fact (not true). For the verb *be,* the common forms of the subjunctive are *be* and *were:* I wish my dog *were* better behaved. My dad suggested that I *be* patient with her. If I *were* more patient, I would train her.

NOUNS

A **noun** is the name of a person, place, or thing.

An **abstract noun** names a quality, a condition, or a state of mind. An abstract noun names something that cannot be seen or touched: *anger, idea, spirit.*

A **common noun** names any one member of a group of persons, places, or things: *queen, city, church.*

A **concrete noun** names a thing that can be seen or touched: *brother, river, tree.*

A **count noun** names something that can be counted: *nickels, bags, emotions.*

A **noncount noun** names something that cannot be counted: *money, luggage, fear.*

A **plural noun** names more than one person, place, or thing: *boys, berries, geese.*

A **possessive noun** expresses possession or ownership.

- To form the possessive of a singular noun, add -'s to the singular form: *architect's.*
- To form the possessive of a plural noun that ends in *s,* add an apostrophe to the plural form: *farmers'.*
- To form the possessive of a plural noun that does not end in *s,* add -'s to the plural form: *children's.*
- To show separate possession, add '-s to each noun: *Meg's* and *Mike's* dogs.
- To show plural possession, add -'s to the last noun only: *Jack* and *Jill's* pail.

A **proper noun** names a particular person, place, or thing. A proper noun is capitalized: *Queen Elizabeth, London, Westminster Abbey.*

A **singular noun** names one person, place, or thing: *boy, river, berry.*

PREPOSITIONS

A **preposition** is a word that shows the relationship between a noun or a pronoun and some other word in a sentence. The **object of a preposition** is the noun or pronoun that follows the preposition: The huge mountain lion leaped *through* (preposition) the tall *grass* (object of the preposition).

A **prepositional phrase** is a phrase that is introduced by a preposition.

- An **adjective phrase** is used as an adjective and modifies a noun: The cabin *in the woods* burned down.

- An **adverb phrase** is used as an adverb and generally modifies a verb: The river flows *into the sea.*

PRONOUNS

A **pronoun** is a word that takes the place of a noun or nouns.

A **demonstrative pronoun** points out a definite person, place, or thing. *This, that, these,* and *those* are demonstrative pronouns: *This* is mine. *Those* are yours.

An **indefinite pronoun** refers to any or all of a group of persons, places, or things. Among the indefinite pronouns are *all, another, both, each, either, few, many, neither, nothing, several, some,* and pronouns beginning with *any* or *every: Each* wants to be on the team. *Both* must pass physicals. *Anybody* can join.

An **intensive pronoun** *(myself, yourself, himself, herself, itself, ourselves, yourselves, themselves)* is used to emphasize a preceding noun or pronoun: I *myself* cooked the entire dinner.

An **interrogative pronoun** is used to ask a question. The interrogative pronouns are *who, whom, which, what,* and *whose:* To *whom* does this belong?

An **object pronoun** is used as the direct or indirect object of a verb or as the object of a preposition. The object pronouns are *me, you, him, her, it, us,* and *them:* Mary called *her* yesterday. Joe gave *them* directions. The call was for *him.*

Personal pronouns have different forms.

- A personal pronoun shows **person:** the speaker (**first person**), the person spoken to **(second person),** or the person spoken about **(third person).** The first person pronouns are *I, me, mine, we, us,* and *ours.* The second person pronouns are *you, yours.* The third person pronouns are *he, him, his, she, her, hers, it, its, they, them,* and *theirs.*

- A personal pronoun shows **number:** it is **singular** when it refers to one person, place, or thing. The singular pronouns are *I, me, mine, you, yours, he, him, his, she, her, hers, it,* and *its.* A personal pronoun is **plural** when it refers to more than one person, place, or thing. The plural pronouns are *you, yours, they, them,* and *theirs.*

- The third person singular pronoun shows **gender:** it can be **masculine** *(he, him, his),* **feminine** *(she, her, hers),* or **neuter** *(it, its).*

A **possessive pronoun** shows possession or ownership. The possessive pronouns are *mine, yours, his, hers, its, ours,* and *theirs.* A possessive pronoun takes the place of a noun and its possessive adjective. Although possessive pronouns show ownership, they do not contain apostrophes: The new skates are *hers.*

A **reflexive pronoun** *(myself, yourself, himself, herself, itself, ourselves, yourselves, themselves)* can be used as a direct or an indirect object or as the object of a preposition: She made *herself* a sandwich. The kitten saw *itself* in the mirror.

A **subject pronoun** is used as a subject or a subject complement. The subject pronouns are *I, you, he, she, it, we,* and *they: We* played soccer. The goalie was *he.*

See also **antecedents, comparisons, sentences, subject-verb agreement.**

PUNCTUATION

An **apostrophe** (') is used as follows:

- To show ownership: the *cook's* hat, the *girls'* horses

- To replace letters or numbers that are omitted: *wasn't, '76*

- With *s* to show the plural of small letters: Mind your *p's* and *q's.*

- With *s* to show the plural of a capital letter that could be misread: *I's*

A **colon** (:) is used as follows:

- After the salutation in a business letter: Dear Sir:

- Before a list when terms such *as follows* or *the following* are used: We bought the following: *eggs, limes, bread, sugar.*

Commas (,) are used to make written material clearer. Among the comma's uses are the following:

- To separate words or groups of words in a series of three or more: We saw elephants, giraffes, hyenas, and monkeys.

- To set off parts of dates, addresses, or geographical names: January 1, 2003; 321 Spring Road, Atlanta, Georgia

- To set off words in direct address: Josie, I'm so pleased that you called me this morning.

- After the word *yes* or *no* when it introduces a sentence: Yes, I agree with you completely.

- To set off direct quotations, unless a question mark or an explanation point is required: "We have only vanilla and chocolate today," he said in an apologetic tone.

- Before a coordinating conjunction in a compound sentence: She called his name, but he didn't answer her.

- After the salutation of a friendly letter and the closing of all letters: Dear Ben, Sincerely,

- To separate a nonrestrictive appositive from the rest of the sentence: Chicago, the biggest city in Illinois, is not the state capital.

An **exclamation point** (!) is used after an exclamatory sentence and after an interjection: Wow! What a celebration that was!

A **hyphen** (-) is used as follows:

- To divide a word at the end of a line whenever one or more syllables are carried to the next line

- In the words for numbers from twenty-one to ninety-nine and to separate the parts of some compound words: *soldier-statesman, half-baked* plan

A **period** (.) is used at the end of a declarative or an imperative sentence and after initials and some abbreviations: Pres. J. F. Kennedy was from Massachusetts.

A **question mark** (?) is used at the end of a question: What time is it?

Quotation marks (". . .") are used as follows:

- Before and after every direct quotation and every part of a divided quotation: "Let's go shopping," said Michiko. "I can go with you," Father said, "after I have eaten lunch."

- To enclose titles of short stories, poems, and magazine articles. Titles of books, magazines, newspapers, movies, TV shows, and works of art are usually printed in *italics* or are underlined: I read "The Lost City" in *Newsweek*.

A **semicolon** (;) is used as follows:

- To separate the clauses of a compound sentence when they are not separated by a conjunction: I can't ride my bike; the wheel is damaged.

- To separate phrases or clauses that contain commas: We went to Paris, France; Rome, Italy; and London, England.

SENTENCES

A sentence is a group of words that expresses a complete thought. A sentence must contain a subject and a predicate.

- An **appositive** is a noun that follows another noun in a sentence and renames it: Kanisha Taylor, the *president* of our class, will make the first speech.

- A **direct object** is the receiver of the action of a verb. A noun or an object pronoun can be used as a direct object: Nat helped *him* with his homework.

- An **indirect object** is a noun or pronoun that tells to whom, to what, for whom, or for what the action in a sentence is done. A sentence must have a direct object in order to have an indirect object: I gave *him* a present.

- The **predicate** tells something about the subject. The **simple predicate** is a verb or verb phrase: Teresa *waved* to the child from the window. The **complete predicate** is the verb with all its modifiers, objects, and complements: Teresa *waved to the child from the window.* A **compound predicate** is two or more simple predicates: Teresa *waved* and *shouted.*

- The **subject** names the person, place, or thing a sentence is about. The **simple subject** is a noun or pronoun: The *man* is riding his bike. The **complete subject** is the simple subject with all its modifiers: *The tall young man* is riding his bike. A **compound subject** is two or more simple subjects: The *man* and the *woman* are riding bikes.

- A **subject complement** is a word that completes the meaning of a linking verb in a sentence. A subject complement may be a noun, an adjective, or a pronoun: Broccoli is a green *vegetable.* The sea will be *cold.* The best player is *he.*

A **complex sentence** contains one independent clause and one or more dependent clauses: *The party had started before we arrived.*

- A **dependent clause** does not express a complete thought and cannot stand alone: *before we arrived.*

- An **independent clause** expresses a complete thought: *The party had started.*

A **compound sentence** contains two or more independent clauses.

- The clauses in a compound sentence are usually connected by a coordinating conjunction preceded by a comma: Sometimes Jane drives to work, *but* today she took the train.

- A semicolon may be used to separate the clauses in a compound sentence: She left on time; the train was late.

A **declarative sentence** makes a statement. A declarative sentence is followed by a period: The sun is shining.

An **exclamatory sentence** expresses strong or sudden emotion. An exclamatory sentence is followed by an exclamation point: What a loud noise that was!

An **imperative sentence** gives a command or makes a request. An imperative sentence is followed by a period: Go to the store. Please pick up the papers.

An **interrogative sentence** asks a question. An interrogative sentence is followed by a question mark: Where is my pen?

A **simple sentence** contains one subject and one predicate. Either or both may be compound. Any objects and/or complements may also be compound: *Ivan* and *John* argued with the grocer. The baby *walks* and *talks* well. Wear your *hat, scarf,* and *gloves.*

Sentence order is the sequence of the subject and verb in a sentence.

- When the verb in a sentence follows the subject, the sentence is in **natural order:** The *settlers planted* the seeds.

- When the main verb or a helping verb in a sentence comes before the subject, the sentence is in **inverted order:** Across the plain *marched* the tired *soldiers.*

See also **clauses, subject-verb agreement.**

SUBJECT-VERB AGREEMENT

A subject and a verb must always agree.

- In the present tense a verb that agrees with a singular noun ends in *-s:* A duck *swims.*

- Indefinite pronouns such as *anyone, anything, everybody, no one, nobody, nothing, one, somebody,* and *something* and indefinite adjectives such as *another, each, either, neither,* and *other* are always singular and require a verb that agrees with a third person singular subject: *Everyone* in this class *works* hard. *Each* girl *is trying* her best.

- Indefinite pronouns and indefinite adjectives such as *all, few, many, several,* and *some* are generally plural: *Few look* carefully before turning. *Both* puppies *are eating* their treats.

- When a sentence begins with *there* and a form of the verb *be,* the subject follows the verb. The verb must agree with the subject: There *is* a *fly* on the wall. There *are bees* in the hive.

- Compound subjects connected by *and* usually require a verb that agrees with a plural subject: My brother *and* sister *are waiting.*

- Some nouns have the same form in the singular and the plural. The sense of the sentence determines whether the subject is singular or plural: Many *deer* live in these woods. A young *deer* is eating the plants in our garden.

TENSES

The tense of a verb shows the time of its action.

- The **simple present tense** tells about an action that happens again and again: I *play* the piano every afternoon.

- The **simple past tense** tells about an action that happened in the past: I *played* the piano yesterday afternoon.

- The **future tense** tells about an action that will happen in the future; the future is formed with the present and the auxiliary verb *will* or the verb phrase *going to* with a form of the verb *be*: The piano recital *will be* on Sunday. I *am going to play* two songs.

- The **present progressive tense** tells what is happening now; the present progressive tense is formed with the present participle and a form of the verb *be:* He *is eating* his lunch now.

- The **past progressive tense** tells what was happening in the past; the past progressive tense is formed with the present participle and a past form of the verb *be:* He *was eating* his lunch when I saw him.

- The **future progressive tense** tells what will be happening in the future. The future progressive tense is formed with the present participle and *will be, is going to be,* or *are going to be:* The teacher *will be grading* the tests this evening.

- The **present perfect tense** tells about a past action that is relevant to the present: I *have lived* here for six years now.

- The **past perfect tense** tells about a past action that happened before another past action: I *had lived* in Memphis for a year before I moved here.

VERBS

A **verb** is a word that expresses action or state of being.

An **intransitive verb** has no receiver of the action. It does not have a direct object: The sun *shone* on the lake.

A **linking verb** links a subject with a subject complement (a noun, a pronoun, or an adjective).

- The verb *be* in its many forms *(is, are, was, will be, have been,* etc.) is the most common linking verb: He *is* happy. They *are* students. The winner *was* she.

- The verbs *appear, become, continue, feel, grow, look, remain, seem, smell, sound,* and *taste* are also considered linking verbs: This *tastes* good. She *became* president.

Modal auxiliary verbs such as *may, might, can, could, must, should,* and *would* are used to express permission, possibility, ability, necessity, and obligation: You *should* hurry. We *might be* late.

A verb has four **principal parts:** the present, the present participle, the past, and the past participle.

- The present participle is formed by adding *-ing* to the present: *walking, running.*

- The simple past and the past participle of regular verbs are formed by adding *-d* or *-ed* to the present: *raked, raked; walked, walked.*

- The simple past and the past participle of irregular verbs are not formed by adding *-d* or *-ed* to the present: *ran, run.*

A **transitive verb** expresses an action that passes from a doer to a receiver. The receiver is the direct object of the verb: The dog *ate* the *bone.*

A **verb phrase** is a group of words that does the work of a single verb. A verb phrase contains one or more auxiliary or helping verbs *(is, are, has, have, will, can, could, would, should,* etc.) and a main verb: She *had forgotten* her hat.

VOICE

In the **active voice** the subject of a sentence is the doer of the action: Betty *wrote* a poem.

In the **passive voice** the subject of a sentence is the receiver of the action: The poem *was written* by Betty.